The American Bicentennial

The AMERICAN BICENTENNIAL

A Cultural History

Lawrence R. Samuel

APPLEWOOD BOOKS

Published by Applewood Books,
an imprint of Arcadia Publishing
Charleston, SC

ISBN 978-1-4290-3043-4

Library of Congress Control Number:
2025934504

For a complete list of books currently available,
please visit us at www.applewoodbooks.com.

Printed in the USA

Contents

Okay guys, one more thing, this summer when you're being inundated with all this American bicentennial Fourth of July brouhaha, don't forget what you're celebrating, and that's the fact that a bunch of slave-owning aristocratic white males didn't want to pay their taxes.

—Ms. Ginny Stroud, high school history teacher, in Richard Linklater's 1993 film *Dazed and Confused*

Introduction

Where were you? I've been asking people of a certain age this question in reference to their physical location on July 4, 1976. Lots of different answers come back, naturally, my own being on Long Island when I was nineteen years old. I distinctly remember watching on television the amazing tall ships enter New York Harbor, a bit regretful now that I didn't go into Manhattan to see them in person.

The American Bicentennial: A Cultural History is, as the title makes clear, a cultural history of the American Bicentennial. With the 250th "birthday" of the United States to take place in July 2026 fast approaching (the Semiquincentennial), it's an opportune time to revisit the country's 200th birthday, which was celebrated 50 years ago. The 1976 event and its 10-year run-up served as a major theme in American culture, crossing over into many different arenas of society. The early 1970s had not been good years for the nation, both economically and politically, something that infused the upcoming event with particular social power and meaning.

The American Bicentennial chronologically traces the controversial evolution of the Bicentennial from its conception in the mid-1960s through its aftermath. The work shows how the event became a key topic in the national conversation and was much more than a one-day celebration (a magnified version of what had taken place a century earlier for the Centennial in 1876). Focal points are how the government used the event for political purposes; how the media and marketers capitalized on it for commercial ones; and how many African Americans had ambivalent and antagonistic feelings toward it. The Bicentennial was of course an ideal occasion to revisit the country's prouder moments of its two-hundred-year past, in the process renewing many of the mythologies that have formed the backbone of our national identity.

The principal argument of *The American Bicentennial* is that despite critics' claims, the event mostly achieved its objective of bringing the American people closer together at a key juncture in the nation's history. The Bicentennial reminded Americans how and why their country was exceptional, while at the same time illustrated the country's shortcomings, particularly in terms of race. With this bold thesis, the work is aimed to be not just the definitive history of the Bicentennial but to offer deeper insights into the American idea and experience.

A brief overview of the work helps set the stage. Chapter 1, "A New Spirit of '76," traces the origins of the Bicentennial between the years 1966 and 1972. Fully aware that the Centennial Exposition in Philadelphia in 1876 had been a popular event during a troubled period of the nation's history, the federal government in the mid-1960s began contemplating an even bigger and better celebration for 1976. President Johnson established a fifty-member commission for such a grand birthday party, soon followed by an act of Congress officially creating what was called the American Revolution Bicentennial Commission (ARBC). Through 1972, however, things did not go smoothly, making many wonder whether the country was going to have its big bash. As well, many African Americans strongly objected to a Bicentennial celebration, accurately pointing out that their historical experience was not at all consistent with the noble ideals expressed by the Founding Fathers.

Chapter 2, "The Powers of the People," examines how the Bicentennial picked up speed in 1973 and 1974. Over the course of those two years, elaborate plans were made on a national, regional, and local level to celebrate what was sometimes referred to as the biggest party in history, a not entirely unreasonable claim given that there would be 218 million attendees (the nation's population). The Nixon administration scrapped the troubled ARBC and created a somewhat new and improved American Revolution Bicentennial Administration (ARBA), redirecting the trajectory of the event. The Nixon and Ford administrations were less than successful in getting the celebration off the ground, but states and local communities across the country were moving ahead with their own plans over those two years. While happenings took many different forms, it appeared that the Bicentennial was serving as a unifying force among many Americans, just as officials had hoped. A significant number of African Americans remained opposed to the event, however, and used the Bicentennial to advance their struggle for equality.

Chapter 3, "A Richly Diverse Mosaic," shows how the Bicentennial (officially set to run from March 1, 1975, through December 31, 1976) quickly became something of keen interest among the media and businesspeople in 1975. Seeing an opportunity to catch the attention of consumers, many marketers eagerly tied into the Bicentennial, heavily commercializing it in the process. Not to be outdone, the federal government heavily promoted the event and licensed its own products. Journalists, politicians, academics (particularly historians), and celebrities all took part in the selling of the approaching event, generating a huge amount of publicity. By now, African Americans were divided on the Bicentennial, with many deciding to recognize the event but not celebrate it. As well, African American organizations found ways to infuse the Bicentennial with Black culture and history, reflecting their dualistic racial and national identity.

Chapter 4, "Hometown U.S.A.," focuses on the Bicentennial in the seminal year of 1976. It was on July 4 that the Bicentennial reached its zenith, making that day an unforgettable one for tens of millions of Americans. I describe the two biggest celebrations—the tall ships sailing into New York Harbor and the array of covered wagons converging in Valley Forge—but also weigh in on dozens of other celebrations held across the United States. Over twelve thousand communities across the country observed the event in some way, establishing the Bicentennial as a rare occasion in which the majority of Americans were united in a common cause. African Americans continued to make their voices heard, however, making the Bicentennial a key site of the civil rights movement.

The brief epilogue explores the disparate reactions to the Bicentennial in 1977 and initial plans for the nation's

Semiquincentennial (250th) anniversary in 2026. Many Americans found the Bicentennial to be a positive experience, although others, particularly many African Americans, were disappointed that little or nothing substantial resulted from it. Couldn't the millions of dollars that were spent have been put to better, more productive use than fireworks? they asked. I contend that despite its overcommercialization, the Bicentennial functioned as a pivot point for the nation's mood, helping bring the country out of its early 1970s funk. While that is far more intangible than social reforms, I argue that the event laid the foundation for the patriotic spirit of the 1980s and, for better or worse, contributed to the formation of a new, more conservative era of national identity.

Sources for the work are primarily period articles published in a wide array of national and local newspapers and magazines. I'm a big believer that journalists really do write the first draft of history, and I owe a big debt to reporters (especially from the *Christian Science Monitor* and *Washington Post*) who covered the Bicentennial beat. Primary materials located at the National Archives, Gerald Ford Library, and Richard M. Nixon Library were sourced wherever possible. Scholarly articles were sourced from JSTOR, and previously published books related to the event helped frame the story.

In addition to those sources, African American newspapers (the *Atlanta Daily World*, *Baltimore Afro-American*, *Chicago Defender*, *Cleveland Call and Post*, *Los Angeles Sentinel*, *Louisville Defender*, *Michigan Chronicle*, *New York Amsterdam News*, *Norfolk Journal and Guide*, *Philadelphia Tribune*, and *Pittsburgh Courier*) are heavily drawn upon. Reporters and columnists for those papers provided a powerful counter-narrative of the Bicentennial that illustrated the palpable tensions that were embedded in the event.

Any study of the American Bicentennial needs to take into account the Centennial Exposition of 1876 in Philadelphia (officially the International Exhibition of Arts, Manufactures, and Products of the Soil and Mine). The exposition, which was the first official world's fair held in the United States, was perfectly timed with the 100th anniversary of the signing of the Declaration of Independence in that city on July 4, 1776, contributing to the fair's significance and popularity. In their *Philadelphia's 1876 Centennial Exhibition*, Linda P. Gross and Theresa R. Snyder showed how the event, which ran from May 10 to November 10, "acted as a catalyst to an expanding national marketplace and growing consumer society." The country was transitioning from a heavily rural, agrarian-based economy to an urban, industrial one, and millions of immigrants were expanding and changing the dynamics of the population.[1]

In his May 1975 article in the journal *The Historian*, Robert Hartje cited a host of problems in the United States during its Centennial that were arguably more difficult to solve than those of 1976. "1876 was a difficult time for celebration as complex issues of post-Civil War America remained unresolved," he noted, yet Americans were somehow able to express optimism during the Centennial.[2] Again, there are strong parallels between 1876 and 1976. The country was reeling in the early 1970s from recent events, notably a deep economic recession, political upheaval, and turmoil surrounding the Vietnam War, filling Americans with self-doubt and a sense that the United States had lost its way. The Bicentennial was seen by government officials and many ordinary citizens as an ideal way to reverse course by celebrating achievements of the past while being the catalyst of a new, progressive future.[3]

Tammy S. Gordon located the American Bicentennial in especially useful historical context in *The Spirit of 1976: Commerce, Community, and the Politics of Commemoration*. The Bicentennial occurred at a pivotal point in the nation's history, she explained, as social, economic, and political forces combined to create a particularly volatile cultural climate. Finding "the spirit of 1976" was thus not an easy thing, yet Gordon concluded that in the absence of a national consensus, individuals and groups were able to make the Bicentennial a meaningful experience.[4] I'm of a similar bent, although I do believe that a certain "togetherness" did take place across the country alongside the more "hometown" nature of the event. (It's important to note that at some point the administrators of the event conceded that the Bicentennial should be more of a localized affair, as a single blockbuster happening failed to materialize for a variety of reasons.)[5]

Beyond the parallels with the Centennial, there are interesting parallels between the Bicentennial and other major events of the nation's past. I hold that the massive effort put forth by the federal government as well as by state and local governments to promote the Bicentennial is reminiscent of the World War II bond campaigns. The FDR administration used bonds not only to raise capital to support the war but also to promote national unity within the context of the nation's increasingly pluralistic society. The Nixon and Ford administrations viewed the Bicentennial in similar terms (i.e., as an opportunity to bring Americans closer together as society split apart along the lines of gender, age, class, race, and sexuality). Not since the early 1940s had the government mobilized its vast resources to shape popular opinion, and corporate America and millions of citizens eagerly enlisted in the celebration.[6] At the intersection of the public and private sectors, the Bicentennial is undeniably one of the key events of the "American century."

The Bicentennial also shares similarities with another major event of the twentieth century—the 1964–65 New York World's Fair. Like that fair, the last major world's fair to be held in the United States, the official history of the Bicentennial is not a particularly favorable one; each event has been attacked by critics for being chaotic and overcommercialized. Such criticism is wholly justified, yet the unofficial history of each event is quite positive. Anecdotally, those who remember the Bicentennial like that world's fair are apt to have a fond memory of their experience, I've found, a prime example of the disparity that often exists between canonized history and public memory.[7]

Even at the time, it was the commercialization of the Bicentennial that virtually ensured that the event would be the target of critics. In one of the most egregious examples, guests could in February 1976 take in the "Star Spangled Bang Bang" act in the Boom Boom Room at the Fontainebleau Hotel on Miami Beach in which a topless woman emerged from a giant birthday cake to the tune of "Happy Birthday America." Following that, a woman dressed as Betsy Ross took off her clothes and pretended to sew them together into an American flag.[8] Four months later, boxers George Foreman and Joe Frazier posed in Bicentennial costumes to hype their June 15 heavyweight match. Foreman dressed up as Sitting Bull, Teddy Roosevelt, General Patton, General Custer, and Abraham Lincoln, while Frazier (who was bearded at the time) went as George Washington, General MacArthur, Ben Franklin, and Betsy Ross.[9] Was it any wonder that the Bicentennial was viewed in less than endearing terms?

In additional to such publicity stunts in highly questionable taste, the Bicentennial was a deep well of material culture, which played out in different ways. One way was through the coins, medals, and stamps that were issued by the Treasury and Postal Service. The themes chosen by the federal government for those coins, medals, and stamps tell us a good deal about the operative "official" cultural values in the United States in the early and mid-1970s. Another avenue of material culture was expressed through the products that were officially licensed by the American Revolution Bicentennial Administration (ARBA) as a means to generate revenue to fund projects. Those artifacts reveal what kinds of things a government agency believed Americans would want to own and by which to remember the Bicentennial.

No laws could prevent marketers from exploiting the Bicentennial as long as the ARBA symbol wasn't used, however, and a steady stream of red, white, and blue products were sold beginning in the early seventies. Such things (which were heavily discounted immediately after Independence Day 1976) reflect the diversity of American free enterprise, i.e., how entrepreneurs are prepared to commercialize a popular event to make a quick buck. (There is actually a Bicentennial Schlock Collection in the Archives at Yale University.) Finally, both professional and amateur craftspeople made their own unique memorabilia to commemorate the Bicentennial, illustrating the ways in which individuals take ownership of a communal event in order to make it personally meaningful.

On that positive note, it's time to tell the fascinating story of the American Bicentennial.

The Bicentennial will forge a new national commitment, a new spirit of '76...which will unite the nation in purpose and dedication to the advancement of human welfare as it moves into its third century.

—President Richard M. Nixon, 1970

1.

A New Spirit of '76

"What's red, white, and blue and brand new from Ford?" asked a 1972 ad from the auto company that ran in many magazines that year. The answer was the Sprint Décor Option Package, which was made available in February 1972 for Ford's three popular small cars—the Pinto, the Maverick, and the Mustang. The "patriotic option group," as it was less formally called, consisted of cars painted white with blue racing stripes outlined in red and American flag shields on the rear fenders. The interiors also carried the all-American color scheme, with blue cloth inserts and red piping in the white vinyl seats. The cars were also being advertised in television commercials with none other than Uncle Sam serving as pitchman.[10]

Why was Ford using the American flag as inspiration for the design of its automobiles during what one could easily say were less than patriotic times? The 1972 Olympic Games were coming up, for one thing, but it was the looming American Bicentennial that made the car company think that there could a market for anything coming in red, white, and blue. This was just the beginnings of what would become an avalanche of consumerism centered on the Bicentennial and just one dimension of the event that critics would find troubling.

The Majestic Significance

It was in the early 1960s that rumblings began for there to be some kind of public recognition of the two hundredth anniversary of the signing of the Declaration of Independence on July 4, 1776. During the Eighty-Eighth Congress, which ran from 1963 to 1964, Representative John O. March Jr. (D-VA) and Representative Fred Schwengel (R-IA) each introduced bills for the creation of an American Revolution Bicentennial Commission. The bills went nowhere, however, and March reintroduced the bill in the following session in early 1965, again not making much of a splash.[11] It wasn't until January 1966, when Representative Charles Mathias (R-MD) and Representative Bradford Morse (R-MA) introduced such a bill that Congress took notice. (Not to be accused of being less than patriotic, Democrats quickly drafted a copycat bill.)[12]

With the anniversary more than a decade away, it wasn't surprising that there had been virtually no initial interest to even discuss something that happened almost two centuries earlier. Beyond the pressing issues of the day, which included troubling events in Southeast Asia, the volatile Cuban situation, the accelerating civil rights and feminist movements, and of course the recent assassination of President Kennedy, the nation had just finished recognizing the one hundredth anniversary of the Civil War. There had been a good number of reenactments of Civil War battles, giving lawmakers a dose of history fatigue. The prospect of twentieth-century Minutemen and Redcoats exchanging musket shots was not a particularly welcome one, nor was the inevitable commercialization of the Revolutionary War and the jingoism that would emerge in the form of anti-Communist dogma.[13]

Revolutionary War–era sites like this one in Hurley, New York, proved to be popular tourist destinations.

Historians were especially worried about how a "bicentennial," as it soon became termed, of the American Revolution could potentially take shape given the nation's insatiable demand for popular and consumer culture. The American Historical Association formed a committee on the matter, making it clear in a report that any commemoration of the Revolution should focus on education and scholarship rather than spectacle and hoopla. Elected officials in Philadelphia, home to the Liberty Bell, would no doubt be tempted to capitalize on the anniversary, the scholars fretted, but so might mayors of thousands of cities and towns where anything related to the Revolutionary War had taken place. The historians' concerns would prove to be justified.[14]

Members of the Academy of Arts and Sciences thought similarly. Upon news that President Johnson was planning to appoint a Bicentennial Commission to select a site for an official celebration of the realization of American independence, the Academy formed its own committee to address the issue. That organization held that a celebration should emphasize "the problems of liberty," both in the past and future. A series of symposia would be best suited for such an intellectual exercise, the committee proposed, considering the president's budding plans for a grand exhibition to be misguided.[15]

As planned, President Johnson asked Congress in March 1966 for approval to create an American Revolution Bicentennial Commission charged with determining how the nation should celebrate the two hundredth anniversary of the 1776 revolution. The commission would consist of four members of the Senate and four members of the House as well as the secretary of state; the attorney general; the secretary of the interior; the secretary of defense; the secretary of health, education, and welfare; the librarian of Congress; the secretary of the Smithsonian Institution; and the chairman of the Federal Council on the Arts and Humanities, along with "seventeen members from private life appointed by the President." The overall aim was to "recall to America and to the world the majestic significance of the Revolution," LBJ told Congress.[16]

The wheels now set in motion, President Johnson announced in July 1966 that he had signed the bill (on the fourth of that month, fittingly) to establish the American Revolution Bicentennial Commission (ARBC).[17] Congress had to authorize funds for anything to happen, however, something not entirely certain despite both parties' flag waving. [18] With more pressing concerns, both domestic and abroad, however, it wouldn't be until the spring of 1969—almost three years after Johnson's signing of the bill—that serious discussion of some kind of celebration reentered the national conversation. By then, a new president was in office, and it was unclear what approach Richard M. Nixon would take to such a thing, if any. [19]

Many Americans, however, were sure that there had to be some recognition of what could be legitimately viewed as the birth of the nation given the magnitude of the occasion. The possibilities were nearly limitless, ranging from Yankee Doodle Dandy–style merriment to a world's fair in Philadelphia or Boston to the kind of history lesson that academics envisioned. The United States had many problems at the end of the 1960s, historians and sociologists made clear, making anything less than an attempt to solve them through a reexamination of the original American idea a missed opportunity. Not happy with how things had been managed by two administrations so far, however, all seventeen "members from private life" who had been appointed by LBJ had resigned, leaving the matter in limbo.[20]

While President Nixon considered new appointees to the ARBC, Boston and Philadelphia officials each put forth their ideas to commemorate the event. Boston planners proposed a world's fair to be called "The Interdependence of Man" and held on a one-thousand-acre site just south of the city's harbor. A megastructure including a floating city inspired by Buckminster Fuller would be constructed on the site, although Uncle Sam would have to kick in at least $250 million to make it a reality. With their imagined world's fair, Philadelphians were taking a different tack, planning to raise the money from private sources and allow citizens to come up with the theme through a national contest. Months went by without comment from the White House, however, leading officials from both cities to think that by putting things on hold, Nixon was trying to "steal" the celebration for Washington, DC. Perhaps they were correct, given that leaders there added their city to the potential sites of a Bicentennial-themed world's fair. [21]

The *Washington Post*, meanwhile, proposed something refreshingly different. Under the banner "Mission '76," the newspaper called for an overhaul of the nation's capital in terms of housing, education, employment, and public transportation, a bold idea by any measure. "The Nation could hardly give itself a better birthday present than a national capital that has demonstrated to its own people and the world that the United States is capable of solving the foremost problem of our time, the problem of the city," editors of the paper had written in 1968, arguing that their city was the logical place to the recognize the events of 1776 in a progressive, socially responsible fashion. (There had been riots in Washington, DC, in April 1968 following the murder of the Reverend Martin Luther King Jr.)[22] Was the run-up to the Bicentennial turning out to be a wrestling match between city boosters?

Apparently yes, given that representatives from the three cities were invited to pitch their respective proposals to a Nixon-appointed commission in July 1969. "The battle of the cities has been raging for months," an editor for the *Washington Post* wrote a week after the first man walked on the moon, with a firm decision to be made by July 4, 1970. Millions, perhaps billions of tourism dollars were up for grabs, this the underlying reason for the intense competition. Keeping its options open, the commission also announced that "people from everywhere" were encouraged to submit their ideas on how the nation should celebrate its two hundredth anniversary. The commission planned to reach out to patriotic, professional, and other organizations to hear what they had in mind, not a bad idea given that the heyday of world's fairs had long passed.[23]

Lawmakers of individual states, however, were not about to wait around for the federal government to figure out how to proceed. In 1969, the state legislature of New Jersey enacted its own American Revolution Bicentennial Bill, appointing that state's historical commission to come up with a plan and allocating a budget of $23,500. The year 1976 would also be the two hundredth anniversary of the first Constitution of the State of New Jersey, additional reason to move forward with or without the rest of the nation.[24]

The presentations given by representatives from Boston, Philadelphia, and Washington, DC, in September 1969 were themselves filled with spectacle and hoopla. Each proposal, however, borrowed from the *Washington Post*'s "Mission '76" by building into the festivities a plan to try to solve or at least lessen the American urban crisis. Boston went all-out, opening its pitch (supported by five New England governors) with a six-man Minuteman fife and drum band. Washington's proposal was endorsed by Maryland's and Virginia's governors while Philadelphia's was backed by those from New Jersey and Delaware.[25] The federal government was planning to award state grants for the Bicentennial, financial incentive for the governors to join forces.

A Big Business Money Grab

As President Nixon's commission mulled over its site selection decision, the Bicentennial was taking shape in various ways regardless of which city would serve as host. (Miami had joined the competition.) In December 1969, the Library of Congress opened an American Revolution Bicentennial Office staffed by professional historians. The mission of the office was to make it known what materials were available to learn about the Bicentennial, what exhibits could be seen, and what special events were being held across the country.[26] In April 1970, the Corporation for Public Broadcasting (parent organization of PBS) asked the ARBC to endorse a planned series of programs on American history, art, and public affairs for the 1972–76 television seasons.[27] The National Endowment for the Humanities (NEH) got involved by granting $37,000 to the American Association for State and Local History, with the money to be used for a study on what kind of programs local historical societies could develop related to the Bicentennial.[28]

By June 1970, the commission had yet to choose a city or concept, running the risk that it wouldn't meet its self-imposed July 4 deadline. Some believed that momentum was slowing for a grand celebration and, more concerning, that there was no real need for one. That month, Wolf Von Eckhardt asked in the *Washington Post*, "After 200 years, is there a spirit of '76?" His answer to the question was "No." "The country is in no mood to plan a big party," he wrote, thinking that all of the cities' proposals were much too ambitious given the money and time that would be required. Plenty of hometown parades, a series of commemorative postage stamps, and a lot of speeches would suffice, Von Eckhardt argued, all of that augmented by an abundant supply of fireworks on the big day itself. Such a celebration was actually more patriotic than a world's fair, he added, and considerably more realistic than the rebuilding of centuries-old, racially divided cities.[29]

Whatever the commission decided, it assured the president and the American people that it would deliver its report on July 4, 1970, as promised. Rumors were that the commission was going to spread the Bicentennial celebration across Boston, Philadelphia, Washington, and Miami, allowing each city to proceed with a scaled-down version of their respective plan. It seemed pretty clear that all four cities were using the event as what Von Eckhardt called "a self-serving Chamber of Commerce promotion," however, and that the Bicentennial would do little to help get the country out of the political, economic, and social mess it found itself in at the beginning of the 1970s.[30]

Undeterred, President Nixon and his supporters decided to make the most of the announcement by labeling July 4 of that year "Honor America Day." Comedian Bob Hope and the Reverend Billy Graham were invited to take part in the festivities in front of the Washington Monument, capped off by a firework show orchestrated by Disney Productions. The recent invasion of Cambodia by U.S. troops and killings at Kent State University had put many Americans, especially young people, in an especially surly mood, making the administration think that such a rally could cheer the country up (and bolster support for the Vietnam War). Things didn't go to plan, however, starting with the arrival of a few hundred war protestors who decided to first have a "smoke-in" during the morning religious service (some joints were colored red, white, and blue) and then take a swim in the Reflecting Pool (many of them were nude). In the evening, police released teargas on the protestors (some waving Viet Cong flags), but the gas spread into the main crowd, creating a sea of weeping people.

What had the ARBC recommended in its first report to the president (Document 91-76 of the second session of the Ninety-First Congress)? While the Bicentennial would be a national celebration (extending from 1970 to 1987, oddly), Philadelphia would serve as the principal host, a fitting decision given that America's independence had been declared in that city. Of course, the nation's capital would play an active part in the celebration, making Washington, DC officials realize they had a lot to accomplish in the next few years. Some thirty-five to forty-five million visitors were expected to come to the capital during the summer of 1976, a number that would overwhelm the city's freeways, parking lots, and Metro system. Doing something about Washington's "ghettos" and "slums" was also vital, as many visitors from across the United States and the world would no doubt be shocked by living conditions just a few football fields away from the White House.[31]

A month after the announcement, President Nixon named David Mahoney chair of the ARBC, replacing J. Wallace Sterling (a former president of Stanford University).[32] Mahoney, president of the conglomerate Norton Simon (and self-described "former drinking and football buddy" of Nixon's), was from New York, but it appeared that he would be spending much of his time in Philadelphia, where a world's fair (or international exposition) in 1976 remained the plan. The fair would be "cultural, inspirational, and patriotic," promised Senator Hugh Scott of Pennsylvania, knowing that the last major world's fair held in the United States (in New York, 1964–65) was widely criticized for being overcommercialized.[33] Washington's celebration would focus on the livability of the city itself; Boston's would trace the history of liberty; and Miami's would present its city as a major trade and cultural center.[34]

Again, however, the ARBC emphasized that the Bicentennial was a national celebration, meaning that the commemoration should go beyond those four cities and the thirteen original states. Bicentennial commissions would be formed in all fifty states, with federal funds made available to make that happen. As well, "citizens whose family roots do not include participation in the Revolutionary War" were encouraged to take part, the first report read, a sensible thing given that the vast majority of Americans in the 1970s were not eligible to join the Daughters or Sons of the American Revolution. The ARBC also proposed three themes that should be woven throughout Bicentennial celebrations: "Heritage '76" (locating our national heritage in its historical perspective); "Open House USA" (educating non-Americans about our history); and "Horizon '76" (urging all citizens to participate in some way).[35]

As soon as Philadelphia was named the host city, it became readily apparent that getting all Americans to join in would present a major challenge. It wasn't yet clear where exactly the world's fair would be located, but African Americans in the City of Brotherly Love were understandably very concerned that creating it in or near their neighborhoods would seriously infringe on their quality of life. Black leaders had earlier charged that homes would be bulldozed to make space for a huge fairground and that the Bicentennial was simply, as Pamela Haynes of the *Philadelphia Tribune* put it, "a big business money grab."[36] African American Philadelphians also felt they had little or no voice in local plans for the celebration and that was in direct contrast to their goal of "self-determination."[37] Such charges, entirely justified given the long history of discrimination toward Black people in that city and the country as a whole, would prove to be just the beginning of Philadelphia's grand plans for the Bicentennial.

A Thin Veil

African Americans' ambivalent feelings toward the Bicentennial were rooted in a long history relating to the recognition of Independence Day. In a speech made on July 4, 1852, Frederick Douglass, the Black abolitionist, asked, "What to the slave is the Fourth of July?" Circumstances for African Americans were much different in the 1850s, of course, but Douglass's thoughts on the issue were insightful not only then but also many years later as the nation prepared for its Bicentennial. For Douglass, July 4 was the day that "reveals to him more than all other days of the year, the gross injustice and cruelty to which he is the constant victim," he stated, proposing that "your celebration is a sham."[38]

Douglass's antebellum view of Independence Day for African Americans was so astute and relevant to events more than a century later that it is well worth repeating more of his words:

> *Your boasted liberty is an unholy license; your national greatness, swelling vanity; your sounds of rejoicing are empty and heartless; your denunciation of tyrants, brass-fronted impudence; your shouts of liberty and equality, hollow mockery; your prayers and hymns, your sermons and thanksgivings, with all your religious parade and solemnity, are to him mere bombast, fraud, deception, impiety, and hypocrisy—a thin veil to cover up crimes which would disgrace a nation of savages.*[39]

Some 129 years after those powerful words were spoken, Ethel L. Payne, a writer for the *Chicago Daily Defender*, reflected on them in relation to the plans being made to celebrate the signing of the Declaration of Independence on July 4, 1776. "If Douglass were alive today, he might not be quite as angry," Payne wrote in August 1971, "but he would be skeptical about the approaching bicentennial celebration of the American Revolution." Payne felt that Douglass would be hardly alone in his skepticism, not looking forward to what would likely be a long series of battle reenactments, pageants in period costumes, abundant fireworks, and "enough patriotism to drown out any guilt about stealing the country from the Indians."[40]

Just as Payne thought, citizens and organizations in many other parts of the country were naturally excited to make plans for how they planned to celebrate the event. Happily, some projects went beyond the stuff of old-timey patriotism. By the spring of 1971, workers at Colonial Williamsburg had their hands full, often quite literally. Researchers at the Carter's Grove Plantation attraction of the visitor center were attempting to grow the varieties of grain, herbs, and vegetables that colonists consumed in the eighteenth century and were even trying to reestablish the breed of cattle that existed at the time. Records of such existed, making the pursuit a challenging but not impossible one. Developing a six-mile gravel carriage road and walking path was also in the works, and the staff was contemplating finding a stern-wheeler or two to cruise along the James River.[41]

The Smithsonian Institution National Collection of Fine Arts also already had its plan in place—a project it was awkwardly calling the "Bicentennial Inventory of American Paintings Executed Before 1914." Locating and photographing as many unknown paintings that were created before that year and were now in public and private collections was the goal, with the information to be stored by computer. The study of American art and artists would be dramatically expanded via the project, the Smithsonian explained, with a 1976 exhibition of the most important found paintings to be the highlight.[42]

Such progress was encouraging, but it was more the exception than the rule. Paul Friedlander of the *New York Times* opined that with regard to the Bicentennial, "there has been progress in a negative way." There would be no world's fair in Boston or Washington, DC, mostly due to local politics, and Philadelphia was still having trouble getting traction for its proposed exposition because of the local opposition and lack of money. Philadelphia planners envisioned a $1.2 billion fair built on air rights over the Penn Central Station in conjunction with a site on the Delaware River at Penn's Landing as well as a third site. There being no takers for such a spectacle, planners slashed the cost to $300-plus million and shifted the proposed site to land near the Byberry State Mental Hospital more than ten miles northeast of downtown.[43]

For Friedlander, the challenge to get anything of magnitude off the ground was as much a matter of timing as money. "This is a poor time to try to focus the attention of America on a Bicentennial celebration of independence and joyous freedom still four years off when there are more than enough contemporary problems demanding urgent resolution," he wrote in May 1971, a not-so-short list of those problems being Vietnam, broke cities with neighborhoods of poverty, a major housing shortage, racial strife, an economic recession combined with high unemployment, and a growing federal budget deficit.[44] Was it any surprise that

Philadelphia and Boston officials were experiencing difficulty getting others to pay for a giant party?

On a positive note, there were other, more manageable Bicentennial-related projects being discussed across the country. $1 million had been raised in Spokane, Washington, to clean up that city's river, a piece of what officials there billed as the "World's Greatest Ecological Exposition." Seattle wanted to restore its waterfront and transform the city's Skid Row into a lovely Central Mall. Arizona wanted to build a 550-acre park near Phoenix "depicting life in the state's pioneer days" that would remain after the Bicentennial.[45]

Given all the false starts and other problems, however, it wasn't surprising that the official start of the "Bicentennial Era" was pushed back to July 4, 1971 (and shortened to 1983), by President Nixon; with five years to go, plans remained vague at best. Critics were already complaining about Nixon's leadership of the event (or lack thereof), particularly with regard to the composition of the ARBC. The commission was indeed stacked with Republicans at the expense of Democrats, with some thinking it was part of his 1972 reelection campaign.[46] (The campaign theme was "Stand Up for America," and Nixon had renamed the presidential jet *The Spirit of '76*.) The Democratic National Committee (DNC) was especially critical of Nixon "stealing" the Bicentennial, saying as much in its *Fact* newsletter:

> *Today the ARBC has no public representatives of American constitutional jurisprudence, American youth, Indian-Americans, American artists, musicians, or dramatists and only one recognized scholar of the American Revolution. The commission and its staff, moreover, are top-heavy with financial contributors to Nixon campaign coffers.*[47]

Controversy surrounding the Bicentennial was continually growing, but that didn't stop the more committed from proceeding with their plans. "Open House U.S.A.," one of the three themes that the ARBC had recommended, was coalescing in the fall of 1971 as members of hundreds of organizations reached out to their counterparts abroad. Fraternal and service clubs, professional and historical societies, civic groups, and international organizations sent letters to contacts in other countries, inviting them to come to the United States during the Bicentennial year of 1976. Some went further by letting foreigners know that they could stay in the formers' homes as guests, a nice showing of hospitality.[48]

The Recreational Vehicle Institute was also acting as a kind host, stating that it would source one thousand campers, trailers, and motor homes for people visiting the country during 1976. The Society of American Travel Writers planned to personally deliver invitations to the Bicentennial in 1974 by turning its annual convention into a round-the-world flying trip. Generating international goodwill was the main aim of such efforts, but it didn't hurt that millions of tourist dollars would flow into the American economy.[49]

Participation from an unexpected group—New Left "radicals"—was also in the making in 1971. "We intend to rekindle the true revolutionary spirit of '76," said activist Jeremy Rifkin in announcing that he and some colleagues had formed the "People's American Revolutionary Bi-centennial Commission." That commission planned to counter the government- and big business–backed ARBC with a considerably less commercial celebration steeped in New Left ideology. "Our feeling is that people are really not too interested in plastic Liberty Bells and giant national birthday cakes," Rifkin noted, thinking there was more value in reminding

Americans of the courageous actions by leftist agitators like pamphlet writer Thomas Paine, Founding Father Dr. Benjamin Rush, and tea partier Sam Adams. American history was in fact filled with radical groups such as the Sons of Liberty, the abolitionists, the barn-burning populists, and labor reformers. For Rifkin, this was the true reason to recognize the signing of the Declaration of Independence.[50]

Rifkin and his fellow radicals were likely happy to hear comments made by Senator Charles Mathias, who five years earlier had been instrumental in the establishment of the ARBC. Mathias felt that the commission had to this point been largely a bust, making little progress in charting a course for a meaningful celebration and failing to include minorities and young people in its planning.[51] Astonishingly (especially given the fact the second wave feminist movement was in full swing), only one woman—Ann Hawkes Hutton, who was actively involved in Washington, DC's Crossing State Park—was appointed to the ARBC by President Nixon.[52]

Such complaints about the lack of diversity of the Nixon-appointed ARBC were well justified. There was originally just one African American among the forty-one members (Dr. Luther Foster, the president of Tuskegee Institute), although a second (Senator Edward Brooke of Massachusetts) was later added. (A Black staffer, Samuel J. Johnson, was also recruited from the Bureau of Census.) There were no Hispanics or Native Americans in the ARBC, and the youngest member, Clarke T. Reed, a Republican senator from Mississippi, was forty-two. The Bicentennial is "not just a time for a party," the Republican senator from Maryland said in December 1971, thinking it was rather an ideal opportunity "for national reassessment of where we are and where we want to go." Jack LeVant, acting director of the ARBC (and former personal care business executive), actually agreed with Mathias, saying that the commission didn't have "any money to do anything." Fortunately, a bill authorizing significant funding for the ARBC had passed in the Senate and was waiting for action to be taken in the House.[53]

Editors for the *Washington Post* concurred with Mathias's opinion that after five years it appeared that what could be said to be the greatest revolution in human history would be celebrated in a decidedly unrevolutionary manner. Flag-waving, coin-minting, speech-making, and song-singing were all well and good, the newspaper's editors observed, but not doing more "would tragically muff a unique opportunity." The newspaper's own "Mission '76" was going ignored, a frustrating thing for those who envisioned a Bicentennial that was both meaningful and lasting. It was true that laypeople were coming up with better ideas than the president's appointees; a group of graduate students and architects in Cambridge, Massachusetts, had come up with "Polis '76," for example, an advanced transportation and telecommunications system for the Eastern Seaboard that promised to improve the quality of life for millions.[54] The high-speed train would travel between Boston and Miami up to 100–150 miles per hour, something quite valuable should the Bicentennial turn out to be a multi-city event.[55]

Clearly responding to the widespread criticism being directed to it, the ARBC took the time to produce a pamphlet that made note of all the progress it had made. Mahoney mailed the pamphlet (titled *Highlights of Progress to Date*) to members of Congress, likely thinking it could convince them to authorize a bigger Bicentennial budget. The list included helping Philadelphia plan an exposition; contributing to Denver's successful bid to host the 1976 Winter Olympics; establishing a stamp committee; designing and adopting an official symbol; and working with a number of states on a Bicentennial seal.[56] With such a paltry list completed over five years, was it any wonder that so many felt that the ARBC should be abolished and replaced with a different group of people?

The Big Birthday Bungle

Plans for the Bicentennial had yet to hit rock bottom, however. In early 1972, it became clear that it was highly unlikely that Philadelphia would be able to pull off its international exposition due to local opposition and cost ($240 million, according to its head, but $1 billion according the ARBC). Opposition was twofold: Black leaders demanded a more prominent role in the planning and some Whites feared a flood of African American workers and "foreigners."[57] On receiving the news that Philadelphia's world's fair was not to be, an editor for the *New York Times* wondered if there should be any national Bicentennial celebration. "It may be that America has become just too old for a birthday party—and too complicated," the rather sad editorial read.[58]

The prospect of there being no keynote event in Philadelphia forced the ARBC to virtually start from scratch, making the six years spent (or not spent) on the project largely a waste of time. Now, it was telling the American people, a truly national celebration was the best way to go about it, specifically through the development of a "Bicentennial Park" in each of the fifty states. The federal government would donate one to five hundred acres in every state, with Washington also to pick up the estimated $23 million tab for design, construction, and landscaping. Congress had to approval this new proposal, of course, with construction to begin in April 1974 if the plan moved forward. There were also ecological studies, environmental impact statements, transportation analyses, and a myriad of other to-dos for "Bicentennial Park" to become a reality, a massive effort requiring great coordination.[59] Was this new and improved plan the best way to celebrate the nation's two hundredth birthday?

Maybe and maybe not, but fifty new parks would hardly be the only products to come out of the coming Bicentennial. Numismatics and philatelists were naturally very excited about the run-up to the event, knowing that there would be new collectables coming out of the U.S. Mint and Postal Service. Indeed, directors of those two agencies were not waiting until 1976 to bring forth Bicentennial-themed coins and stamps. In April 1972, for example, it was announced that four new stamps featuring colonial craftsmen—a glassmaker, a silversmith, a wigmaker, and a hatter—would be issued on July 4 of that year in Williamsburg, Virginia. The eight-cent stamps (the cost of mailing a first-class letter between May 16, 1971, and March 2, 1974) included the wording "Bicentennial Era," just the kind of thing that philatelists loved for their collections.[60]

Collectables were certainly nice, and there would be many of them for the Bicentennial, but Americans were expecting something much bigger, even if it didn't have lasting social value. Knowing that there was little chance that Philadelphia would have its world's fair, officials in Boston were in 1972 putting together something it called "Prologue '75," a scaled-down international exposition. Its theme was "The City Is the Exhibit," meaning Boston itself was the exposition, an interesting (and less costly) approach. Preempting the 1976 celebrations was also an intriguing decision; there might be smaller crowds but also less competition for tourist dollars.[61]

Again, however, federal funds would be required to produce "Prologue '75," something not at all assured. Given the projects bring considered—extending the Boston Freedom Trail, developing a Boston Naval Shipyard Historic Park at Charlestown, reconstructing Bunker Hill Monument and Monument Square, creating Liberty Tree Park to surround the Liberty Tree, building a Tea Party Commemorative Park in Fort Port Channel, and fixing up Fort Independence on Castle Island—"Prologue '75" would not come cheap.[62]

In May 1972, the proposed Philadelphia fair was officially scuttled by the ARBC (by a vote of 23 to 4, with presumably 14 abstainers), but that didn't seem to drum up much interest in "Prologue '75." The tide was definitely turning toward holding many celebrations in all fifty states versus a single bash in one city, with the price tag of the latter playing a big part in that shift.[63] Philadelphia officials began to think what it could and should do using city and state funds, with the federal government perhaps chipping in a bit. "There is no time for weeping and wailing," an editor for the *Philadelphia Tribune* wrote after hearing the vote, thinking the city would still celebrate in style.[64]

The national media took note of what had taken place, however, thinking that some crying might be in order given what a debacle it had been. "A large crack has been noticed both in the Liberty Bell and in the city's self-image," Ellen Kaye wrote for *Harper's Bazaar*, with precious little to show for the $3 million that had been spent on master plan after master plan. Infighting and power plays made Philadelphia appear like a scene of a Second Revolution, she observed in her piece, with hardly any agreement among locals on how the event should be recognized. Betwixt the nation's capital and the Big Apple, Philadelphia was said to already have an inferiority complex, and this latest kerfuffle only made residents feel worse about their hometown.[65]

The collapse of the Philadelphia fair was just one aspect of what Eugene L. Meyer of the *Washington Post* called "the big birthday bungle." Commercialization of the event, which many had warned would happen, had already begun, much to the dismay of Meyer and others who hoped that the Bicentennial would be more than a colossal marketing opportunity. Ford was running its TV commercials featuring an Uncle Sam pitching red, white, and blue cars; the popular symbol of the U.S. government wanted to see many of the autos driving "over purple mountains' majesty, amber waves of grain." (The voiceover for the commercials imitated all-American John Wayne's recognizable way of speaking.) Meyer understandably worried that this was just the beginning of four more years of patriotic consumerism as big business coopted the Bicentennial.[66]

Permission to use the visual logo of the event—a "red-white-blue pretzel" for Meyer—was much sought, as it served as an official endorsement by the U.S. government. (The theme of "One nation bound in unity" went along with the symbol.) Many big corporations had approached the ARBC, asking that they be allowed to put the symbol in advertising or on packaging, as it could be worth millions of dollars in extra revenue. (Lipton, for instance, wanted to host a "gala high tea party" in Boston.) The commission was proceeding cautiously in this regard, however, trying to figure out the degree to which they should license the logo (in exchange for payment, of course). So far, just the Mount Rushmore and Niagara Falls tourism boards, the National Medical Association, and the 1976 Winter Olympics in Denver had received authorization to use the logo in their promotions.[67]

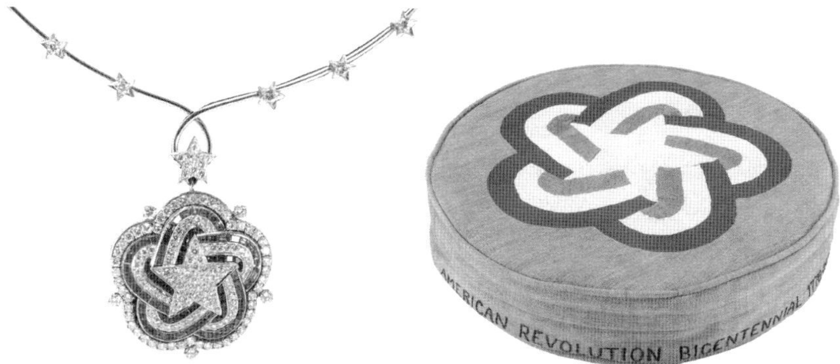

LEFT: Critics of the Bicentennial logo may not have seen this necklace made of rubies, diamonds, and sapphires set in white gold, which had a detachable pendant that could be worn as a pin. The unworn piece, featuring thirteen stars, was made by well-known jeweler Pierre Touraine. RIGHT: A blue pillow featuring the Bicentennial logo. The stitching along the side reads, "American Revolution Bicentennial 1776–1976."

While obviously well-intentioned, the Bicentennial had taken on different meanings for different groups rather than a single one grounded in a celebration of American independence. Leftists saw it as a demonstration of consumer capitalism and an ironic violation of the country's revolutionary beginnings; many African Americans viewed it as a travesty of claims of liberty, democracy, and equality for all; Democrats complained that it was just a political ploy; and even some who leaned decidedly right felt that it was excessive self-praise. It was marketers who took the (birthday) cake, however, exploiting what could be seen as a sacred event for profit.[68]

Even some Republicans expressed criticism of the Nixon-appointed ARBC, which was loaded with pro-business conservatives. Mathias, who had already voiced his displeasure of how the Bicentennial had been managed, called the group "basically a stuffed-shirt committee" and commented that he felt "a little like a father whose child has gone astray." Representative Fred Schwengel (R-IA), who had chaired the Civil War Centennial

Commission, urged that LeVant be fired, calling his leadership "woefully inadequate." Mahoney had asked John D. Rockefeller III to create a youth advisory committee, but all twenty-five members selected refused to serve on it. "Your commission represents no one in this country," their message to Mahoney read, adding that "it is composed like the exclusive social club it is."[69] Getting the message (and thinking it could help more Black voters), Nixon named eight new members of the ARBC, including three African Americans: Roy Brooks, a twenty-two-year-old pre-law senior at the University of Connecticut; Vernon Jordan, the new executive director of the National Urban League; and Charley Pride, the country music star.[70]

A State of Incipient Failure

The People's American Revolutionary Bicentennial Commission was naturally disapproving of the ARBC (it used an Uncle Sam clock as its logo), adding to their historical list of true revolutionaries Davy Crockett (who as a congressman tried to get rid of West Point) and Helen Keller (a devout Socialist and unionist). Along the lines of the People's American Revolutionary Bicentennial Commission, two brothers from Cleveland had decided to take matters in their hands by proceeding with how they believed the event should be recognized. The men, Robert and Vincent De Forrest, had formed the Afro-American Bicentennial Corporation, saying that members of the ARBC "obviously were not doing any meaningful Bicentennial projects at all." The brothers actually succeeded in getting grant money from the Department of Housing and Urban Development (HUD), the National Park Service, and a few foundations to create "programs with meaning for thinking Americans and black Americans." Their group had organized a conference of African American scholars in Washington, DC, in January 1972, with their work focused on restoration of a slave cemetery in Georgetown.[71]

The backstory of the creation of the Afro-American Bicentennial Corporation was rather remarkable. Vince De Forest had previously worked for the Atlanta-based Southern Christian Leadership Conference, while Robert had just returned to Washington after an Army tour in Vietnam. Upon seeing how the Bicentennial was taking shape via the ARBC, the brothers paired up to fill the glaring gap in terms of African American participation. Seeing that their organization was making progress in a way that the ARBC likely never could, Mahoney personally reached out to the De Forests to "promote programs to improve the quality of life of black and other minority Americans in conjunction with the Bicentennial." Soon a national conference billed as "What the Bicentennial Should Be to the Black People of the United States" was held, with a series of regional and local meetings planned.[72]

In addition to the restoration of the abandoned slave cemetery in Georgetown (which included graves of British soldiers), the Afro-American Bicentennial Corporation had a number of other projects in the works, including a multimedia Afro-American educational and cultural center emphasizing the connections between African Americans and countries in Africa and the Caribbean. The De Forests had formed an advisory board whose members were drawn from local communities, politics, academia, and religion, as well as from the worlds of sports and entertainment. (Singer Roberta Flack was one such member.)[73]

A year later, the Afro-American Bicentennial Corporation launched an exciting project in concert with the Interior Department and the National Park Service. (In February 1971, President Nixon had directed those areas of the federal government to stir up Americans' interest in their historic and cultural heritages.) Twenty leading scholars of Black history urged that the nonprofit corporation pursue the study, the goal being to identify those sites that most deserved to be designated National Historic Landmarks (places considered to possess national historic significance). Congress provided the funds for the project, which was divided into three areas: development of the English colonies (1700–75); political and military affairs; and society and social conscience. The findings from the study were to be published in a book.[74]

Undeterred by the escalating criticism of the ARBC, Nixon went ahead with his plans for the Bicentennial by inviting people around the world to visit the United States at some point during the next four years. "This is the time to open our hearts and our homes and our communities to those who come to America for the first time," the president said on July 4, 1972, in a national radio broadcast delivered from his home office in San Clemente. Formal invitations would go out soon to foreign government officials, a means of improving international relations as American involvement in Vietnam continued. The Bicentennial was an opportunity for Americans to tell people of other nations "you helped to make us what we are" and urge them to "come and let us say thank you."[75]

Such pleasant political rhetoric could not compensate for the findings from a study conducted by a consultant firm hired to assess the performance of the ARBC. The commission was "in a state of incipient failure," Cambridge, Massachusetts–based Arthur D. Little reported in July 1972 after its investigation, finding "resentment and low morale" among the ARBC's staff and no clear goals. (The ARBC had itself commissioned the study.) The firm took special aim at LeVant, who told the media that much had changed since the evaluation, which was done five months earlier. The House had not surprisingly just rejected the ARBC's request for $6.7 million in funding for a full year, but the Senate Judiciary Committee appeared to be in favor of it.[76] Before it made its decision, however, the Senate Judiciary Committee planned to hold public hearings on the matter in August, making the July release of the report very bad timing for the ARBC.[77] At this rate, was there going to be a Bicentennial?

Given how things had gone since 1966, the answer to that question wasn't clear. "Just when planning for the nation's bicentennial should be gaining steam and support," wrote an editor for the *Washington Post*, "the American Revolution Bicentennial Commission has plummeted in public and congressional esteem." Americans differed greatly on how the Bicentennial should play out, but seemingly everyone agreed that those who were in charge of it were incompetent. Worse, the way that things had been managed appeared to affect Americans' feelings about the Bicentennial in general, adding to what some were calling the nation's "malaise."[78] Just one day after that editorial ran, Jack LeVant resigned from his post as the director of the ARBC. (David Mahoney, the commission's chair, stayed put.) Mahoney praised LeVant in accepting his resignation, telling the media that Congress's decision to withhold needed funds was the real problem.[79]

One might have thought that plans for the Bicentennial had by that point hit rock bottom, but woes continued to mount.

Native Americans joined the chorus of faultfinders, demanding they play a larger part in its conception. The National Congress of American Indians, which represented 250,000 members of 145 tribes, condemned the ARBC in a press conference and at the Senate Judiciary Committee (actually a subcommittee). African Americans and women had previously protested about their respective lack of representation on what was now a 50-member commission, and the fact that there was a single Native American on it made this latest objection entirely understandable and justified. The group demanded greater representation on both the ARBC and on the state Bicentennial panels.[80]

Of course, given the history of the United States, Native Americans had a special interest in how a Bicentennial played out. Celebrating the past, which would no doubt be a central theme of the event, was inappropriate, Clydia Nahwooksy, a Cherokee and director of Indian awareness at the Smithsonian Institution, told the Senate. Celebrating the present also seemed wrong based on the current status of Native Americans and the Inuit and Aleut people, she added, recommending that the Bicentennial be about achieving greater ethnic awareness and rectifying injustices.[81]

In response to criticism that women were underrepresented in Bicentennial planning, the ARBC in February 1972 formed the Women's Coalition Task Force (WCTF) as part of the commission. (The task force came about after Wilma Scott Heide, national president of the National Organization of Women [NOW], told Mahoney just that.) The WCTF, which was made up of about twenty different women's groups, was attempting to build a national network of "community resource centers" for women. Representatives from NOW, the National Spanish Speaking Women's Caucus, the American Association of University Women, the General Federation of Women's Clubs, B'nai B'rith Women, and the League of Women Voters were included in the WCTF.[82]

Although it remained unclear what these community resource centers would actually do and who would staff them, the general idea was to determine how women could contribute to and participate in the Bicentennial. Recognizing women's role in the history of the United States was another main goal. "We want to speak to the past, particularly to show the women of America what accomplishments women in the past have made—accomplishments which have gone largely unrecognized until now," said Cathy Irwin, a member of the WCTF and president of the Washington, DC chapter of NOW.[83]

Against the backdrop of the feminist movement, it could be seen how the WCTF wanted equal representation in all Bicentennial events. "If they are going to put up statues of famous Americans," Irwin told the *Los Angeles Times* in August 1972, "let's make sure famous women are among them." Other initiatives the WCTF were pondering were an encyclopedia of American women; a multimedia traveling show promoting women's achievements and contributions; and a television series about women in American culture. "We are also thinking of helping to revise children's textbooks to put women in their rightful historical perspective," Irwin added.[84]

In addition to its lack of inclusiveness, there had long been allegations that the ARBC was heavily politically motivated, and in August 1972, documents were produced that proved it. Jeremy Rifkin of the People's American Revolution Bicentennial Commission along with Erwin Knoll, Washington editor of *The Progressive*, had somehow obtained records demonstrating that Republicans were using the Bicentennial in a partisan manner.

Feminist groups seized the Bicentennial as an opportunity to fight for equal rights.

It was an election year, of course, making political promoters look for opportunities to shape the opinion of Americans in their party's favor. In the most egregious example, Dr. J. Max Bond, an African American Republican, was appointed to a special advisory panel of the ARBC strictly on the basis of his potential ability to, as one document read, "help blacks better understand and relate to the Republican Party."[85]

Also as suspected, commercial interests were deeply embedded within the ARBC's culture, according to the same set of documents. But what would one expect with a chairman who was the head of a company that owned other companies, including Canada Dry, Hunt-Wesson Foods, and Somerset Importers (in the liquor business)? Food concessions would be present at the fifty Bicentennial Parks the ARBC had proposed be created, and there was hard evidence that ARA Services, which sold food to arenas, stadiums, and racetracks, was attempting to influence Mahoney's decision about what brands would be sold at them (specifically Canada Dry, Hunt-Wesson Foods, and Somerset Importers).[86]

Innocent enough, perhaps, given the way that business worked, but there was no doubt that the ARBC asked Congress to allow it to make contracts with suppliers without having to go through the standard government practices of open and competitive bidding.[87] Such machinations, and even more so the politically motivated ones, were enough reason for the House to kill the bill that would provide a $6.7 million budget to the ARBC. Going further, the chair of the House Judiciary Committee ordered a top-to-bottom investigation of the commission, as it became clear there was much funny business going on and little actual planning.[88]

The General Smell of the Thing

Professional historians' lukewarm at best opinion about the approach the commission appeared to be taking toward the Bicentennial did not help the ARBC's cause. Since the very beginning in the mid-1960s, historians had made it clear that scholarship should be prioritized over spectacle, and this hadn't changed. "Almost everything that has happened so far has not been intellectually respectable," said Robert K. Webb of the American Historical Association soon after the snub by Congress. Webb had in fact testified at the Senate subcommittee, going so far as to say that he and his colleagues wished the Bicentennial could just "go away" due to the "meaningless rituals and rhetoric" that were bound to be seen and heard over the next few years. By the 1970s, Americans were capable of understanding that their history went beyond "simple-minded myth," Webb added, something that the ARBC couldn't or refused to recognize.[89]

Alongside such boosterism, the "Bicentennial Papers," as the exposed documents had been nicknamed (after *The Valachi Papers*), revealed that the ARBC was a (literal) old boys' club whose members got jobs for friends and did favors for local districts. The commission had rebuffed anything left of center or potentially controversial, choosing instead to reach out to the likes of the Miss America contest and the Orange Bowl parade as sponsors. In short, the ARBC merged public and private interests, perceiving the American people more as consumers than citizens. "The situation cries out for reforms," the *Washington Post* declared, predicting that there would be a major overhaul of the commission now that its misdeeds had become common knowledge.[90]

Senator John Pastore (D-RI) put his assessment of the situation less diplomatically. "I don't like the general smell of the thing," he stated in announcing that he was resigning his seat on the ARBC. (He was one of four senators on the commission.) As others had said, the commission was running much too loosely, and its members "don't really know what's going on," adding to Senator

Fred Harris's (D-OK) conclusion that the ARBC's actions were "a theatrical sham." Other senators, including Ted Kennedy (D-MA), agreed, thinking that there was too much going behind the scenes and not enough in front of the public.[91] A Republican member of the ARBC, Representative Lawrence Williams of Pennsylvania, defended the commission, however, saying that the attacks were made by "a group of liberal Democratic senators."[92]

Just as feared, the Bicentennial was clearly becoming a heated and divisive political issue rather than a uniting force among the American people. The congressional Black Caucus (thirteen Black congressmen, all House Democrats) joined the chorus of critics, warning African Americans to "exercise extreme caution and be aware of the manipulative practices of the politically motivated ARBC." Not just Blacks, but "ethnic groups, academicians, women, and youth" were being left out of the planning process as the interests of big business and Nixon's reelection campaign took priority.[93] In September 1972, one member of the Black Caucus, Representative Parren Mitchell (D-MD), had the opportunity to address the ARBC at its quarterly meeting. Jeremy Rifkin was present (reading from the internal documents for forty-five minutes), as was Clydia Nahwooksy, each of them highly critical of the commission.[94]

The ARBC might have simply decided to call it quits right there, but at the end of that meeting, it voted to make changes in response to the barrage of criticism. The changes were adding two more congressional members (one from each party) to its executive committee; giving the full forty-nine-member panel more power; raising the number of congressional meetings from four to six; and adding three more members of the public to the executive committee, all from minority groups.[95] Could these steps save the ARBC and rescue the Bicentennial from the dustbin of history?

It appeared so given the remarkable meeting that soon took place. Like two world leaders trying to reach détente, Rifkin and Mahoney formally met for the first time to see if their vast divergence in view could be somehow bridged. On the surface, at least, the two men were nearly as different as could be: the twenty-seven-year-old Rifkin's salary at the People's American Revolution Bicentennial Commission was $60 a week, while the forty-nine-year-old Mahoney reportedly earned $350,000 a year as CEO of Norton Simon. (He received no pay as the chair of the ARBC.) Interestingly, however, the men had grown up in working-class families and attended the University of Pennsylvania's Wharton School (where they both won the prestigious Award of Merit). It was unclear whether anything substantial would result from the fascinating get-together, but each man was impressed by his adversary. "I'd rather spend my time with Rifkin than in 17 meetings on Capitol Hill," Mahoney said. Rifkin acknowledged, "I must admit there was some rapport there."[96]

The mutual admiration between Mahoney and Rifkin didn't stop the House Judiciary Committee, led by Representative Emanuel Celler (D-NY), to move forward with their "in-depth" investigation of the ARBC. (The General Accounting Office was also involved.) Rather than pleased about that, however, Rifkin considered it "disgusting," thinking that the documents he obtained spoke for themselves.[97] A month or so later, the investigation had gotten underway, but the ARBC decided on its own to revamp its organization. Basically, the commission voted to streamline itself by eliminating many responsibilities and decreasing the number of staff members. The move was an admittance that the ARBC was trying to accomplish too much with what it claimed to be a lack of resources.[98] The trimming didn't stop the ARBC from coming up with a budget of $12.4 million—almost double the $6.7 million it had been seeking—although it was almost certain that Office of Management and Budget (OMB) and Congress would make cuts has they had in the past.[99]

In putting together its budget, the ARBC seemed to get the message that it should focus more on scholarship and partner with various government agencies, including the NEA, the National Trust for Historic Preservation, and the Smithsonian.

Money was allocated for the following:

- ★ One hundred American studies awards "to encourage young scholars to pursue innovative approaches to our heritage"
- ★ Twenty prizes for books on the American revolution
- ★ A "heritage memorabilia search" in which ordinary Americans would comb through their attics, basements, and barns for Americana, the most interesting of which would be donated to museums
- ★ Restoration of fifty-five historic buildings to be used as meetinghouses for local citizens
- ★ A "multiethnic" folklore troupe totour the country in 1976
- ★ Holding of Liberty Day '76 to be held over the July 4, 1976 weekend, primarily in Washington and Philadelphia
- ★ Artist workshops and training sessions
- ★ Invitation USA, in which foreign artists, craftsmen, and interpreters would be brought over in 1975; and
- ★ A seed bank for endangered plant and flower species

Bicentennial planners in Philadelphia were following the same route by scaling back expectations and taking a more targeted approach. In place of a sprawling $1 billion exposition, the organizers were now working toward developing programs based on three specific themes—the city's historic role, foreign participation, and the urban environment—which would cost a much more reasonable $75 to $375 million. Mayor Frank Rizzo was actively involved in this new plan, knowing that, even without the Philadelphia Expo, tourists would still be keen on seeing where it all happened two centuries earlier. The ARBC and the president would have to give their blessing, but that seemed likely since Rizzo (despite switching parties to Democrat) was a strong supporter of Richard Nixon (who was likely to get reelected the following week).[100]

The more realistic plans being made in Philadelphia and by the ARBC were signs that Bicentennial planners were finally recognizing the constraints that lay before them. Mistakes had been made, something the General Accounting Office made clear in its investigation of the ARBC. The commission had overpaid consultants and staff members, the GAO's December 1972 report stated, and learned that the ARBC went over budget by $124,650. (Another discovery was that LeVant had improperly received more than $2,000 in "living expenses.") Overall, however, the ARBC had done a good job, according to the GAO, a much more positive appraisal than that made by many others.[101]

The report issued by the House Judiciary Committee a week later was considerably less kind. Based on its performance to date, the ARBC would not be able to provide the nation with a "meaningful" Bicentennial, the committee concluded after its investigation, with lots of ideas tossed about but little of substance produced. Simply put, the ARBC had no real vision of what the Bicentennial celebration should be, making it not surprising that there was minimal progress made. For six years, the commission spent most of its time examining its own role in the event, not a very productive use of time and money. The House Judiciary Committee called for a reorganization of the ARBC that encouraged a clear definition of its role, as without it the commission would "continue to founder...in its current haphazard fashion."[102] The American Bicentennial was now just three and a half years away, not a lot of time to prepare to commemorate what many believed was the most significant event in the history of nation. Not surprisingly, more challenges lay ahead in the country's ambitious effort to create, as President Nixon had envisioned, a new spirit of '76.

All across the country, thousands of Americans have been meeting and planning for the Bicentennial—in places which were never touched by the drama that took place two centuries ago.

—Los Angeles *Sunday Herald-Examiner*, December 1974

2.

The Powers of the People

There was trouble at the state reformatory in LaGrange, Kentucky, a couple of weeks before Christmas 1973. Was it a prison break? It was not. Rather, the state's Bureau of Corrections reported that it was not going to be able to deliver the number of Bicentennial license tags that the director of Prison Industries had promised. There was a shortage of steel and paint due to the energy crisis, affecting production of the special plates that would be sold through each county's Bicentennial committee for two dollars each. Some 105,000 Kentuckians had placed an order for one of the license plates, but it appeared that many of them would be disappointed to hear that they wouldn't be receiving one.[103]

Of course, the Kentucky license plate snafu was small potatoes within the context of the seven-year history of the nation's Bicentennial. One didn't have to be an expert to see that the management of the event to date had been, in a nutshell, a mess. The clock was ticking toward July 4, 1976, and by the beginning of 1973, there was still no definitive "master plan" regarding how the nation would recognize its birth. There were too many cooks in the kitchen, many would say, as individuals and organizations attempted to use the event to further their own agenda. It was clear that things needed to change, and change fast, if the country was going to have the celebration it deserved.

A Matter of Spirit

The year 1973 did not get off to a particularly good start for the ARBC when leaders of various minority groups got the chance to speak to Congress about how they viewed the Bicentennial. Planning for the event should shift toward education, social reform, and community involvement, members of the African American and Native American groups insisted, the concern being that their respective histories would be misrepresented or omitted without the redirection. Representative Parren Mitchell had arranged the meeting to get the criticism into the open, saying that he planned to ask the Black Caucus to vote against additional funding to the ARBC unless its scope became more inclusive.[104]

Happily, President Richard Nixon was among those who could perceive the exclusive and dysfunctional way that the Bicentennial had been handled during his and the previous administration. In February 1973, news came that the president planned to propose legislation in Congress that would scuttle the now fifty-member ARBC and replace it with a single Bicentennial "czar" whom he would appoint (with advice and consent of the Senate). That person would appoint his or her own deputy, another means of staying on point. Going further, the chosen administrator would be given the power to skirt the usual government procedures, thus avoiding the bureaucracy and red tape that had plagued the process. While there would be a twenty-five-member advisory board (with no Congressional members), the members would be appointed by the president and report to the administrator. The ARBC had canceled its upcoming scheduled meeting, a sign that something big was indeed looming.[105]

Such legislation was proposed the following week. Nixon told Congress that the new organization would result in "a more streamlined, tightly organized, and action-oriented structure," but the *Washington Post* expressed skepticism that it would right the floundering ship. "Much more than good management and tight scheduling will be required to salvage the bicentennial during the next three years," the editors of the newspaper wrote, thinking that the key to was more "a matter of spirit" that a reorganization.[106]

Members of Congress were more than skeptical of the president's plan. A House subcommittee did not like the idea of an "all-powerful" administrator at all and strongly objected to his or her ability to bypass the usual procedures regarding contracts with secondary parties. The chair of the subcommittee, Representative Harold Donohue (D-MA), wondered aloud whether the president was seeking "absolute and dictatorial powers" regarding the course of the Bicentennial (prompting a White House spokesman to reply, "Not at all").[107]

While politicos fought over control of the American Bicentennial, citizens made their own plans regarding how they would like to observe the event. The Arnold Expedition Historical Society had come up with an especially interesting idea: a wilderness trek through rough terrain in Maine and Quebec, tracing the steps that Benedict Arnold had made two hundred years earlier. Arnold, the military officer who had risen to the rank of major general in the Continental Army before defecting to the British in 1780, had led more than one thousand American soldiers along the 335-mile route in a failed attack on Quebec City. The march occurred before Arnold became the most famous traitor in U.S. history.[108]

The planned trek was an ambitious one and illustrated how the Bicentennial meant quite different things to different people. Half of the 1,150 men (the same number of Revolutionary War soldiers) would board 220 boats (again, the same number used) at Pittston, Maine, in September 1975, and paddle along the Kennebec River, the beginning of what would be a four- to six-week journey. (The other half would walk along the banks as Arnold's men did.) From there, the trip was on land, following what were described as "ancient Indian trails." The Arnold Expedition Historical Society, the sponsor of the journey, made it clear that it was a historical and conservation organization and had no desire to venerate Arnold.[109]

The thousand or so devoted Continental Army reenactors would hardly be the only ones tracing the steps of Revolutionary-era would-be Americans. "Hordes of tourists will be zeroing in on American Revolution bicentennial activities in 1975 and 1976," proclaimed the *Christian Science Monitor* in April 1973, with New England to be where most of those hordes would visit. New Englanders themselves were ambivalent about hosting millions of tourists from near and far, appreciating the revenue that would come into the area but at the same time concerned about the possible damage they might cause to historical sites. Travel operators in England, Germany, and Japan were heavily promoting trips to New England in 1975 and 1976, making some locals worried there would be a foreign invasion that would overwhelm the hospitality business. If one wanted to follow the

New England Heritage Trail (which crossed through six states in the region), Ralph Hubley, travel editor of the *Christian Science Monitor*, advised, it would be wise to beat the crowds by going in 1973 or 1974.[110]

Boston, not surprisingly, was aggressively courting tourists for its upcoming Bicentennial celebration, which was planned to begin on April 19, 1975 (the two hundredth anniversary of Paul Revere's ride announcing the British advance on Lexington and Concord). The city had come up with the name "Boston 200" to brand its offerings, which mostly involved visitors walking various trails of historical significance, particularly the red brick Freedom Trail. The Black Heritage Trail included a stop at the site of the Boston Massacre, where Crispus Attucks, who was formerly enslaved, was among the first colonists to perish in the cause for freedom.[111]

While Boston's official Bicentennial kickoff was two years away, the city was planning to get a head start in mid-December 1973, the two hundredth anniversary of the Boston Tea Party. Many hotels were already fully booked for much of 1975 and 1976, making a visit to Boston Harbor for that commemoration a good (if chilly) option, given there might be no room in the inn during the peak of Boston 200. The city's chamber of commerce was telling those unable to book a hotel room to look into alternatives such as college dorms, frat houses, campgrounds, and even military barracks. Airbnb was decades away, but the chamber was suggesting that Bostonians might want to rent out their homes during the busiest season, as that had been somewhat successful at Montreal's Expo 67.[112]

Vermont and New Hampshire, meanwhile, were busy making their own respective plans for the coming rush to New England.

(New Hampshire was one of the original thirteen colonies, but it wasn't until 1791 that Vermont joined the new republic.) Vermont's government had asked officials in the state's 251 communities what they had in the works, if anything, so that promotion of such could be scheduled. Ski resorts across the state were planning for an influx of visitors who wanted to take in the amazing scenery during the summer of 1973 and were getting ready their chairlifts, aerial tramways, and gondolas.[113]

The fact that cities and states were moving ahead with their own initiatives was a good thing given that no national celebration had yet to be agreed upon. In 1972, the ARBC had squashed the 1976 Philadelphia World's Fair, and in May 1973, it squelched the overly ambitious and costly Bicentennial Parks concept under pressure from various federal agencies and the White House. Congress too was against it because of the estimated price tag ($1.3 billion), instead leaning toward offering matching grants to states, territories, and the District of Columbia for their own programs falling within the umbrella themes of Heritage 76, Horizons 76, and Festival USA. Funds for such were envisioned to come from the sale of Bicentennial medals to the public, although a lot of medals would have to be sold to raise the money needed.[114]

The ARBC, which was still alive despite Nixon's proposal to appoint a Bicentennial czar, was embracing this approach by redefining its mission. Rather than come up with a single big idea, the commission decided it would instead assist local organizations with putting in place their own celebrations. To do that, however, more staff was needed, and the ARBC asked a House subcommittee to authorize increasing the number of its employees from 100 to 144. (Regional offices were planned to be set up.) Until it was made clear whether the ARBC would even exist, however, it made little sense to set aside funds to add to its staff.[115]

The *Washington Post*, as usual, weighed in on this latest development, and lamented that there would be no fifty-state Bicentennial Parks program. The editors mused that while state and local programs were fine, it would still be nice to have some kind of national one as, after all, "the American Revolution created one nation." To that point, just as the newspaper proposed its Mission '76 idea some years back, now it suggested as a nationwide Bicentennial theme elevating the Interior Department's anti-litter campaign to "a more comprehensive environmental clean-up." The ecological movement was indeed heating up in the early seventies, making the editors think a massive cleanse of the country's water and land would be well worth the effort.[116]

Pathways to Celebration

In some sense, there was a national Bicentennial program in place through the new coins and stamps that were being issued by the federal government. The release of both coins and stamps was usually scheduled for the Fourth of July of a particular year. In 1973, for example, a block of four postage stamps commemorating the Boston Tea Party was issued by the U.S. Postal Service, one of a number of Bicentennial-themed releases planned. Each of the stamps featured a scene of the 1773 event in which angry colonists dumped chests of tea from British ships into Boston Harbor to protest the English-levied tax. The four stamps carried the inscriptions "The Boston Tea Party, U.S." and "Bicentennial Era" as well as "8c" (the cost of mailing a first-class letter was eight cents at the time).[117]

Such efforts by the federal government were certainly worthwhile to get Americans "Bicentennial-minded," but something much bigger was overshadowing that effort. President Nixon had formally kicked off the five-year Bicentennial era on July 3, 1971, at the National Archives (where the Constitution and Bill of Rights were kept), but now, two years later, the Watergate scandal had seriously damaged his public

Speaker of the House of Representatives Carl Albert, President Richard Nixon, and Chief Justice Warren E. Burger kicking off the Bicentennial Commemorations at the National Archives on July 3, 1971.

Vice President Nelson Rockefeller; Mrs. Robert MacNamara, the chairman of the Reading Is Fundamental program; Dr. James B. Rhoads, U.S. archivist; and John Warner, the head of the ARBA at the National Archives, on Constitution Day in September 1975. Children from the RIF program attended the ceremony and were given a tour of the Rotunda by the vice president.

standing. News of the burglary and wiretapping of the DNC headquarters by members of Nixon's reelection campaign and the subsequent cover-up (which would lead to the president's resignation in August 1974) had stalled Bicentennial plans and were serving as a major distraction. The Bicentennial was intended to serve as one of if not the highlight of Nixon's presidency, but things were turning out much differently than planned. The transgressions attached to Watergate were "clearly not what the founding fathers had in mind when they framed the Constitution and the Bill of Rights," Eugene L. Meyer noted in July 1973.[118]

Watergate might have had something to do with John D. Rockefeller III taking the time to offer a lesson in the past, present, and future of the United States to an audience at the University of Arkansas on the two hundredth anniversary of Parliament's passage of the Tea Act. The act subsequently led to the tea party and Revolutionary War, something that had major relevance today, according to the head of the Rockefeller Foundation. The country was now in the early stages of what he called the "Second American Revolution," he explained, with a number of movements that had surfaced or escalated over the last decade—the counterculture, civil rights, women's liberation, environmentalism, and consumerism—all part of this second revolution. Rather than being an economically stagnant, socially traumatic, and politically chaotic time, Rockefeller proposed, it was an exciting time for Americans. "I see the Second American Revolution as a positive and promising social force," he stated, countering critics who maintained that the country was in decline and had lost its way.[119]

Six months later, S.I. Hayakawa, working for the Nixon administration, also made a point that things were not as bad as they seemed as the Bicentennial neared. Life expectancy was a lot longer than it was at the turn of the twentieth century, for one thing, this despite all the worrying that pollution and pesticides had poisoned the water, air, and land. The "good old days" were not that great, Hayakawa reminded readers of *Saturday Evening*

Post, many of them no doubt nostalgic for a simpler time. Crime, drug addiction, and prostitution were all more prevalent a century earlier, putting the concerns over those very same social ills in historical context. Child labor was common, and there were no government safety nets for those unable to support themselves. Many diseases had been controlled or conquered, and racism, while still a big problem, was not nearly as bad. And while many major cities were going through tough times, the urban landscape of the turn of the century was by no means a paradise. Horse dung littered the streets, and every year thousands of the animals were abandoned when they dropped dead, spawning disease. "I'll take carbon monoxide," Hayakawa remarked, thinking life at America's centennial was considerably worse than at its Bicentennial.[120]

Jeremy Rifkin saw things much differently, thinking America was not in a good place in the 1970s. As the name of his group made clear, Rifkin wanted little or no governmental involvement, believing that it was the American people themselves who should manage the event and in a progressive fashion. (The man kept a "Don't Tread on Me" flag in his office, complete with coiled snake.) The People's Bicentennial Commission had gained broader support since Rifkin released the revealing ARBC documents, even working with the Smithsonian Institution on a planned folklife festival and with the National Council of Churches and the Day Care Council of America on other initiatives.[121]

Rifkin and his supporters were no doubt not pleased in the fall of 1973 when the idea of what was being called "The American Bicentennial Fleet" was, well, floated. It had appeared that the ARBC was resigned to simply help administer state and local programs rather than orchestrate a major national event after all of its proposals had failed to take shape. That assumption seemed to be not entirely true after the Federal Maritime Commission (FMC) pitched the concept of the American Bicentennial Fleet to the ARBC, however.[122]

The plan for the American Bicentennial Fleet involved about forty flotillas visiting at least fifty ports all over the world, the FMC explained, its cost of nearly $1 billion to be covered by corporate sponsors and visitor tickets. The fleet would consist of many different kinds of ships, floating pavilions, barges, and assorted Navy, Coast Guard, and Merchant Marine vessels, and would sail the world between April 1, 1975, and October 2, 1977. More than 237 million people would witness the fleet, the FMC added, a number that exceeded the entire population of the United States (203 million, according to the 1970 Census).[123]

Was such a thing feasible? Given that the American Bicentennial Fleet was designed to be a global event, this concept was arguably more ambitious than any of the previous big ideas that the ARBC had pondered. It was the many smaller ideas that better represented the country's interest in the Bicentennial in the run-up to 1976, however. Historical societies were naturally committed to launching some kind of program, although many of them simply didn't know what theirs should be and how it should be executed.[124]

Happily, a new book called *Bicentennial USA: Pathways to Celebration* was published in 1973 to serve as a resource for such societies and similar organizations. The guide, which was authored by Robert J. Hartje and published by the American Association for State and Local History, was to help planners create programs that would "open up the human capacities of America to the highest degree," the guide boldly stated. Case studies from past celebrations (including those in Canada) were included, as were tips on fundraising and generating publicity. Most important, Hartje advised planners, strive for more than the three Ps—picnics, pageants, and parades—as Americans deserved a deeper exploration of their heritage than such superficial fare during this once-in-a-lifetime event.[125]

The Reverend Paul J. Asciolla concurred. Asciolla, the editor of *Fra Noi*, an Italian American newspaper based in Melrose Park, Illinois, believed that "U.S. history needs an overhaul" and suggested that this endeavor should be the focus of the Bicentennial. Asciolla envisioned forming a commission of the preeminent scholars and social commentators whose mighty task would be write a "serious study of America and its people, its past, and its future." He conceded that such a monumental work would not likely be able to be completed in just a few years, but it could begin, a superior alternative to the "series of sickening park dedications, street-naming ceremonies, parades, and parties" that were otherwise likely on the way. No such work existed, according to Asciolla, and current scholarship did not adequately address such critical aspects of American history as the immigrant experience, intergroup relationships, class conflict, the labor movement, and the story of African Americans.[126]

Historians would likely to have been pleased to learn of what was said to be the first Bicentennial Cultural Exchange Program. The program, which was facilitated by the Braintree (Massachusetts) Historical Society, involved students from Hillcrest Junior High School in Philadelphia and Central Junior High School in Braintree. Twenty-five students from each school visited historical sites in the other school's host city, an interesting exercise that definitely went beyond the three Ps. Interested families opened up their homes to the visiting students and drove them around to the chosen sites, a great example of how ordinary Americans were already investing the Bicentennial with meaning.[127] "Official plans in Washington for the coming bicentennial may be proceeding at a snail's place," observed Mimi Mead of the *Christian Science Monitor*, "but elsewhere they are booming."[128]

Less than an hour away by car from Braintree, however, planners were thinking about how to prevent visitors from experiencing the Bicentennial. Town managers in both Lexington and Concord, Massachusetts, were planning to block incoming traffic after a designated number of people had entered each area to relive the "shot heard 'round the world." Drivers would be instructed to visit any of the many other historic sites of the Bay State once that point was reached. Many of the locals, meanwhile, were planning to spend as much of 1975 and 1976 somewhere, anywhere else than the area where the American Revolution had begun on April 19, 1775, with the exchange of gunfire between British troops and colonial militiamen.[129]

While the battle that had been waged between twentieth-century Bostonians and Philadelphians in the competition to win the main event of the future Bicentennial had subsided, reverberations of it could still be felt. America was born in Philadelphia, officials of the City of Brotherly Love told their counterparts in Beantown, in what was a friendly yet intense rivalry in laying claim to the birth of the nation. Philadelphia '76 Inc., which was the latest Bicentennial committee in that city, was attempting to acquire the $100 million in federal funds it had been promised by the White House. As usual, however, how the city planned to spend that money remained unclear, with some making the reasonable case that rather than throw a lavish party, it should be used to improve the school system, attack the drug problem, improve race relations, and provide more jobs.[130]

Some Philadelphians knew exactly how they intended to commemorate the Bicentennial. The Philadelphia chapter of the Hymn Society of America was taking the lead in writing new hymns—religious songs of praise to God—that reflected core elements of the nation's identity, such as thanksgiving for God's guidance of the country, individual freedom, and the pursuit of material wealth. A panel of judges would choose the best Bicentennial hymns and have them published, set to music by composers, and then distributed to churches throughout the English-speaking world.[131]

New hymns may not have been what one would think first about the Bicentennial, but the Philadelphians appeared to have a better grasp of the meaning of the event than planners in Boston. As announced, Bostonians held another tea party in December 1973 to commemorate the one that had taken place there two hundred years earlier. Many historians recognized the original Boston Tea Party as the catalyst for the revolution and ultimately independence, but its reenactment was not well received by critics. Not only was it "contrived and artificial," thought Stephen Isaacs of the *Washington Post*, but the 1973 version also was "distinguished by commercial and ideological hucksterism that seems pandemic to this land today." Salada Tea rather than Lipton had received rights to partner in the restaging, and the public had to pay admission to board the *Beaver II* brigantine to watch the proceedings (in which no tea was actually contained in the tossed boxes for ecological reasons).[132] It was safe to say that the course of the American Bicentennial had been charted.

A Chain Reaction

A couple of weeks prior to the less than revolutionary Boston Tea Party, a small item appeared in that same newspaper offering more evidence that a new direction had been set for the Bicentennial. On December 11, 1973, President Nixon signed legislation creating the American Revolution Bicentennial Administration (ARBA) to replace the ARBC effective January 1974. It authorized $20 million in funding, with the ARBA to consist of an eleven-member board led by a full-time administrator. The president, still embroiled in the Watergate fiasco, also made it clear that planning for the nation's two hundredth birthday had to be accelerated.[133] A couple of weeks later, Nixon accepted "with regret" the resignation of David Mahoney, ending the latter's three-year tenure as chair of the ARBC. The president had yet to appoint the administrator of the new ARBA.[134]

In March 1974, Nixon named Secretary of the Navy John Warner to head up the ARBA. The president, who was at his Key Biscayne villa at the time, delivered the news via a coast-to-coast radio broadcast. "We can build a future in which, a hundred years from now, another anniversary can look back with pride on a time when our generation ensured for them a world at peace," he said, adding that the theme of the Bicentennial was now "The Spirit that Built America." Nixon made mention that he instructed Warner, who had been the Navy secretary for about a year and a half, to soon provide a master plan of the event to his cabinet. This time around, the president made clear, any and all other appointments made would be "completely nonpartisan," seemingly trying to repair some of the damage caused by Watergate.[135]

For columnist James J. Kilpatrick, the appointment of John Warner meant that the Bicentennial was "back on course." In fact, the appointment had regretfully not happened two years earlier, as much more would have been achieved if the president had made the move back then. Warner (who claimed to be "completely non-political") was stripping the ARBA from partisanship, according to Kilpatrick, and the former understood that nongovernmental sources of revenue were necessary if the Bicentennial was going to be something more than a bunch of parades down Main Street USA. Still, given all the obstacles laying ahead in the next two years, Warner "will have brought off a miracle of public administration" if the Bicentennial turns out to be a success, Kilpatrick thought.[136]

Warner made it clear in interviews with the press that he (like Jeremy Rifkin) had no interest in the Bicentennial relying on a world's fair or endless series of pageants to be successful. Rather, like many scholars had argued, the event should be an opportunity for Americans to take a close look at their heritage and institutions to better appreciate their value. And rather than use the Bicentennial to try to distract citizens from Watergate, Warner thought it should be addressed in the event's plans, as it showcased American democracy at work. When pressed to be specific about such plans, however, Warner was decidedly vague. "It has an aura of mystery," he confessed to a reporter for the *Atlanta Constitution*, although the man did have his own interpretation of what it should be about. "The Bicentennial means to me doing something so that you leave your country in a little better shape than when you found it," Warner stated, which was as intelligent as anything that had ever been said about it.[137]

In his March 1974 radio address, President Nixon had set the celebration of the country's Bicentennial to officially begin in March 1975, giving Warner a full year to get his house in order.

Although it appeared that there now would be some kind of national event organized by the ARBA, Nixon made clear that the Bicentennial belonged to the American people. "We shall seek to trigger a chain reaction of tens of thousands of individual celebrations," the president stated, again an attempt to improve his public image by presenting the Bicentennial as a shining example of democracy. In fact, as part of what his aides had named "Operation Friendly Persuasion," Nixon would make public appearances in Chicago, Nashville, and Houston the following week to achieve the same objective. Impeachment proceedings were moving ahead in the House, impetus for the president to do whatever he could to stay in office.[138]

One of the more interesting of those tens of thousands of individual celebrations was promised to come not from an American but a Canadian. Captain George Molecey of the Royal Canadian Mounted Police Veterans' Association in Barnaby, British Columbia, offered to bake not one but six birthday cakes, each weighing 200,000 pounds, to celebrate the American Bicentennial. Molecey was not a professional baker but had successfully produced a 30,000-pound cake to commemorate the Mountie Centennial, suggesting he might have been able to actually pull off this larger feat. Still, given the ingredients required for each of the mammoth cakes—70,000 pounds of flour, 40,000 pounds of raisins, 20,000 pounds of pineapple, 10,000 dozen eggs, 32,000 pounds of sugar, 17,000 pounds of pecans, 24,000 pounds of cherries, and a "pinch" (2,000 pounds) of salt—Molecey may have been biting off more than he could chew. The ex-Mountie had not decided on how the cakes would be decorated, the more obvious choices being the *Mayflower*, Betsy Ross, the Declaration of Independence, the Liberty Bell, and busts of all the U.S. Presidents.[139]

Molecey's plan to bake half a dozen football field–sized cakes was an indication of the turn the Bicentennial was taking as 1976 drew increasingly near. Perhaps because no grand public celebration had materialized, individuals and organizations were starting to come forward with all kinds of rather peculiar ideas to recognize the event. While Molecey's proposed scheme was extraordinary, if more than a little farfetched, what might be called Bicentennial kitsch was rapidly finding its way into the marketplace. Bicentennial ashtrays, plastic Liberty Bells, musket-shaped liquor bottles, and faux pewter everything represented just a small sample of what was being sold and presumably bought.[140]

Those in the business of marketing such products saw nothing wrong in capitalizing on the Bicentennial. In fact, missing out on the opportunity would be a big mistake, as this excerpt from a trade magazine called *The Specialty Salesman* made clear:

> *If you're looking for money, the bicentennial can be the biggest bonanza in your lifetime.... It's not too early to be thinking about how to cash in on the coming wave of patriotism, the likes of which we may not see for another 200 years.... Every man, woman and student will be a "red, white and blue" prospect. Come the Revolution, profits are sure to be fast, furious, and fantastic.*[141]

For author and journalist August Heckscher, such zeal was entirely predictable given the ways of American-style capitalism. "From now through 1976, in a thousand ways—many of them no doubt odd, marred by commercialism or greed," he wrote for the *Christian Science Monitor* in April 1974, "we shall be marking the birth of the United States."[142] Since the wheels of the Bicentennial were first set in motion in the mid-1960s, critics and historians had consistently bemoaned marketers' exploitation of it. But in a way, its commercialism was very much consistent with the roots of the American Revolution. Scholars such as Charles Beard had convincingly argued that the Founding Fathers had economic self-interests in mind when conceiving their new nation, suggesting that profit-motivated pitchmen of the twentieth century were simply carrying on our capitalist tradition.[143]

So was, apparently, the ARBA, judging by its decision to attend a June 1974 conference in Chicago designed to show business people how to connect their products and services to the Bicentennial. The ARBC had been attacked for endorsing commercialization of the event, making one wonder why this new administration was seemingly following the same course.[144] Representative Henry Reuss (D-WI) urged the ARBA to not only refuse to take part in the upcoming conference, but also "disavow" it and "denounce the types of promotional tie-ins that will be discussed there and do everything in its power to prevent this travesty of American heritage." It was one thing making use of what the private sector excelled in, Reuss wrote in a letter to the ARBA, but, he added, if anything will cheapen the bicentennial, it is plastic George Washingtons or Minutemen ashtrays imprinted with company names and slogans."[145]

Extending Charles Beard's thesis, would Jefferson, Franklin, and Hamilton have approved of Americans cashing in on a wave of patriotism two centuries in the future? Perhaps, but it was good to know that there would be more substantive elements of the Bicentennial. There would be something called an "American issues forum" attached to the Bicentennial, the federal government announced in June 1974, its goal to prompt citizens to discuss specific problems facing the country. The NEH would develop the forum in concert with the ARBA, with a ten-member panel to help plan the weekly conversations. CBS News anchor Walter Cronkite, who would serve on the panel, conceived the idea for such a forum. "Our aim is to encourage a national dialogue deeply rooted in a better understanding of our history," said Donald Berman, chair of the NEH, in announcing the forum, something that must have made many academics happy to hear. (Professors from Columbia, Harvard, and Stanford Universities were included on the panel.)[146]

Cronkite likely had something to do with television producers at his network and the others deciding to create and air Bicentennial-themed content. NBC had in the works an adaptation of Carl Sandburg's classic biography of Abraham Lincoln, and PBS was putting together a show on the Adamses. CBS was going positively Bicentennial happy, producing 732 "Bicentennial Minutes" that started running on July 4, 1974. Each sixty-second segment was a morsel of American history narrated by a notable figure. In one, legendary actor Charlton Heston spoke George Washington's words upon hearing news of the Boston Tea Party, while in another, Jean Stapleton (then playing Edith on what was the country's most watched television show, *All in the Family*) read Martha Washington's formula to keep cherries from spoiling.[147]

While television viewers enjoyed this lighter fare, an "American issues forum" could not come at a better time for William H. Stringer. Writing for the *Christian Science Monitor* a month after the forum was announced, Stringer held that, "In this time of Watergate affairs, Americans need to be reminded of the wellsprings of their country's greatness." Discussing the nation's current problems within the context of its remarkable history was as good as any way to celebrate the Bicentennial, he believed, echoing the thoughts of previous socially minded critics. For

Stringer, however, it was America's future that mattered more than its past. "Where is the U.S. heading? Where is the world heading?" he asked, the answers unclear in what was without question a troubled period of American history.[148]

The Buy-Centennial

Two years before its July 4, 1976 climax, more details of the American Bicentennial were becoming clear. Although there wouldn't be a single giant bash, many exciting celebrations across the country were taking shape. "Tall ships" from some thirty countries would arrive in New York Harbor on Independence Day 1976, it was being reported, apparently a downscaling of the overly ambitious "American Bicentennial Fleet" concept. (It appeared that there simply wasn't enough steel in the world to build such a massive fleet.)[149] A definitive encyclopedia of American Indians was going to be published, it was also announced, and the Smithsonian Institution was going to hold a series of folk festivals and open a new museum dedicated to air and space. The Smithsonian's National Portrait Gallery was already displaying Revolutionary-era paintings and artifacts in no fewer than eighteen rooms, a truly tour de force show.[150]

While all those were prominent observances, it was the hundreds of modest efforts that perhaps even more so reflected the Bicentennial spirit. Whether in progress or in the planning stages, local communities were diving into their past, even if they didn't date to the eighteenth century. Civil War buffs seemed just as excited as anyone about the coming Bicentennial and justifiably so given the role of that tragic event in the nation's two-hundred-year history. Even some World War II enthusiasts were comparing FDR and the various five-star generals to the Founding Fathers through the latter's efforts to preserve democracy from fascism and totalitarianism.[151]

Still, the stars of the Bicentennial show were unequivocally those associated with the War for Independence, particularly the seven principal Founding Fathers (Washington, Jefferson, Franklin, Hamilton, John Adams, John Jay, and James Madison). Along with the minting of new coins to commemorate the Bicentennial was a discussion in Congress whether the $2 bill, which had featured Thomas Jefferson, should be reissued in some form. (The bill had been discontinued by the Treasury Department in 1966 due to lack of public demand.) Representative Jerry L. Pettis (R-CA) had in June 1974 introduced a measure that would have the Treasury bring back the Jefferson $2 bill with a Bicentennial theme on the reverse. (Such a bill was indeed issued in 1976, with the reverse incorporating a reproduction of John Trumbull's 1818 painting of the signing of the Declaration of Independence.) Victor A. Holt, a Washington, DC cab driver, had led a vigorous but ultimately unsuccessful campaign for the Treasury to produce a $2 bill featuring Dr. Martin Luther King Jr. on the front in place of Jefferson.[152]

In 1974, it was, however, the Smithsonian Institution that was going all out for the Bicentennial. In additional to the National Gallery of Art paintings and new air and space museum, the Smithsonian was going on the road with something called the *Manuscripts of the American Revolution* exhibit. This was the first Bicentennial-related project developed by the Smithsonian Institution Traveling Exhibition Service (SITES) and was targeted to historical societies. Included in the exhibit were thirty documents and letters chosen by the Manuscript Society, which

The construction site on the plaza in front of the West Building of the National Gallery of Art, Washington, DC.

was and remains the oldest society of autograph and manuscript collectors in the United States. (It has since expanded to be an international organization.) Visitors to the exhibit could see documents relating to the Stamp Act of 1765 and the election of President George Washington, as well as letters by Samuel Adams, John Hancock, Nathanael Greene, and others. For those historical societies that either couldn't afford to show the original documents or couldn't provide adequate security, facsimile copies were made available at a reasonable cost.[153]

The Smithsonian's traveling exhibit was a smart way for the institution to connect with the many Americans who would not be able to get to the nation's capital over the next couple of years. A tour of the country revealed that many states were implementing their own plans with regard to the Bicentennial as very broadly defined. On Kodiak Island in Alaska, for example, residents chose as their "new" community meetinghouse an eighteenth-century log building that had originally been used as the storehouse of a Russian-American company. California was focusing on the 1848–55 gold rush, with its redwoods now known as "Liberty Trees," while Montana was organizing an open-range cattle roundup. Hawaii, meanwhile, was emphasizing its unique culture but also trying to increase voter registration to 100 percent by 1976.[154]

If one had to name a single community in the United States that was struggling to identify a course of action for its Bicentennial, a good case could be made that it was, ironically, Washington, DC. (Philadelphia would give DC a good run for its money but was stepping its game, notably by volunteers' restoration of Old Fort Mifflin.)[155] Federal plans for the nation appeared to be on track or at least moving in that direction, but locally, things remained rather a mess. Talk of a Fort Lincoln model community had stalled, as had a proposed Eisenhower civic center and a new Federal City College campus. Likewise, the envisioned social programs to improve the city's quality of life had made little progress, in part because Washington's local Bicentennial Commission hadn't met for months. (No one could even say with certainty who was on it.) In that commission's defense, just a fraction of the money it had been promised by the White House and Congress had been delivered, quite a problem given that some thirty-five million tourists were expected to visit the capital city in the summer in 1976.[156]

A few thousand miles away, elected officials and private interests in Los Angeles were attempting to put together "Pacific 21," which was described as "a gala international exhibition and festival focusing on the Pacific nations." A number of cities on the East Coast had failed rather miserably in their respective efforts to develop a world's fair–type event for the Bicentennial, but that didn't appear to discourage these West Coast hopefuls. Pacific 21 would run through the summer of 1975 in the Century City area, according to its organizers, with a number of countries, including Chile, the Republic of China, Malaysia, and Korea, allegedly already having reserved space. Corporate sponsors like Alcoa were behind Pacific 21, not too surprising given its goal of "promoting new cooperative efforts between nations of the Pacific in business, trade, and other forms of economic activity in the last quarter of the century."[157]

Efforts by Corporate America to appropriate the Bicentennial to serve its own interests led Wolf Von Eckhardt of the *Washington Post* to coin a new term: the "Buy-Centennial." "The commercial exploitation of the nation's 200th birthday has already begun," he observed in August 1974, making note of some of the ways in which the Bicentennial was being turned into the Buy-Centennial. California-based Liberty Ice Cream had, for example, created a brand called America's BiCentennial Ice Cream, the flavors being Valley Forge Rum Raisin, Mount Vernon Cherry Pecan, and Yankee Doodle Double Fudge Marble. Retailers were being told by consultants to add something of colonial vintage to their store displays to build traffic. (A bed slept on by George Washington scored extra points.) General Motors had followed AMC and Ford with its Bicentennial limited-edition automobiles; magazine ads for the "Spirit of America" Chevrolets included a cobblestone road and a woman in colonial-era clothes.[158]

Judging by the showrooms of souvenir manufacturers, much more of this would be coming over the next two years, Von Eckhardt warned. Crockery, mugs, key chains, pillowcases, and even thermometers were emblazoned with a drum and fife corps or some other symbol of the American Revolution. In addition to the inexpensive kitsch, there was fine bone china plates bearing the likeness of figures like Abigail Adams, Patrick Henry, and Thomas Paine. Limited edition copies of George Washington's inaugural sword in sterling silver could be had as well as reproductions of his "personal pistols."[159]

Was all this as terrible as it might sound? Hucksterism of one sort or another had been part of everyday life in the country for as long as anyone could remember, making Buy-Centennial just the latest and perhaps largest expression of the hawking of snake oils during the first medicine shows (which actually took place in colonial times). One might even argue that Archibald Willard's revered painting *The Spirit of '76* (created for the 1876

A safe used for the 1876 Centennial that President Ford opened a century later.

Centennial Exposition in Philadelphia) was in its time a kind of kitsch, making that being produced a century later just carrying on a long American tradition. (Thousands of lithographed copies of that painting were sold, making art dealer J.F. Ryder rich.) For Von Eckhardt, the corporatization of the Bicentennial could be detected in its symbol; while his *Washington Post* colleague Eugene L. Meyer saw it as a red, white, and blue pretzel, Von Eckhardt opined that it "might as well be the emblem of the Chase Manhattan Bank."[160]

Where It Belongs

The ARBC and then the ARBA had never established a definitive policy regarding use of that symbol, but in August 1974, the latter finally did. The ARBA would license use of the official Bicentennial symbol to those manufacturers of souvenirs and commemoratives that met standards set by that administration. (The standards included being of American manufacture, possessing relevancy to the Bicentennial, meeting a high level of both quality and safety, having national distribution, and carrying a reasonable price.) In exchange, royalties would be paid to the ARBA, with the money used to help support its projects. Beyond generating a revenue stream, the ARBA's decision was to retain greater control over the unofficial Bicentennial products that had flooded the market, many of them less than tasteful.[161]

With the resignation of President Nixon in August 1974, there was a general sense that a new era in American history had begun and that the country's Bicentennial had been given new life.[162] There was a new ARBA board under President Ford, but John

Warner remained its head. It was highly unlikely that marketers would resist attempts to capitalize on the Bicentennial, whether authorized to do so or not, but it appeared that there would be greater effort put forth to construct events of which Americans could take genuine pride.

Right on cue, it was soon announced that a main feature of the Bicentennial would be a reenactment of a wagon train complete with fifty Conestoga and prairie schooner wagons (copies of the originals, with modern improvements) pulled by teams of Morgan horses and driven by college seniors. (There would be an additional ten supply wagons.) The "Bicentennial Wagon Train Pilgrimage" would make its way across the country from Los Angeles starting on January 1, 1976, and bivouac in Valley Forge, Pennsylvania, on July 4 of that year, where it would then encamp for three months. State and federal grants would cover the estimated $5 million cost, a lot of money but considered well-spent if the pilgrimage succeeded in reminding Americans of their pioneer spirit.[163]

Another cross-country trek was in the planning stages but would use a much different vehicle. Beginning in May 1976, the more adventurous and physically fit would be able to take one of two different bicycle routes starting on the Oregon coast and ending in Washington, DC. Tour leaders, marked roadways (in participating states), and a guidebook listing places to stay and repair shops were included in what was being called the "Bikecentennial '76." Was there a better way to see the country? bicycle enthusiasts asked, the answer a firm "No" for the three to five thousand cyclists who made the 3,500-mile trip each summer. (The first one took place in 1884 on a decidedly non-aerodynamic two-wheeler.) The ARBA had given its blessing to the project, as had the U.S. Department of Transportation (for being 100 percent nonpolluting). Over the course of anywhere from forty to eighty days, cyclists would pass through a dozen states and skirt all major cities, offering a firsthand view of the "real" America.[164]

Yet another form of transportation would go coast to coast as part of the nation's celebration of its Bicentennial. The American Freedom Train would pull out of Boston in April 1975, the beginning of a twenty-one-month journey. The twenty-four cars were painted red, white, and blue, naturally; inside, each car contained artifacts, documents, and other materials featuring highlights of American history (including a slave bill of sale, a film of Babe Ruth hitting a home run, and a lunar rover). Funded by corporations and private individuals, the train powered by a steam locomotive would pass through forty-eight states and make, fittingly, seventy-six stops.[165]

Plans had also materialized for a representation of the Bicentennial overseas. There had long been talk of such a thing, as the event served as an ideal vehicle of international diplomacy. In November 1974, the ARBA announced that *The World of Franklin and Jefferson* would be shown in Paris, Warsaw, and London throughout 1975. The 7,500-square-foot exhibit, which included photographs, documents, and memorabilia relating to the pair of Founding Fathers between the years 1706 to 1826, would return to the United States in 1976 for shows in New York, Chicago, and San Francisco.[166]

The first official export of the American Bicentennial was groundbreaking in another way. *The World of Franklin and Jefferson* would be the first time that a private corporation helped fund a Bicentennial project; given all the discussions between the ARBC and ARBA with various companies, it was amazing that it had taken so long for that to happen. IBM was donating $500,000 toward the project, which was designed by architect Charles Eames and his wife and staged by the New York's Metropolitan Museum of Art. The ARBA and its predecessor had always been short of money due to Congress's justified concern about the state of Bicentennial planning, and John Warner was now determined to change that by partnering with the private sector. "One of our specific objectives is to stimulate contributions in dollars and planning," he plainly put it.[167]

The lives of Franklin and Jefferson were exceptional, however, and some Bicentennial planners were more interested in the everyday lives of ordinary colonists. Re-creating daily life in the late eighteenth century would offer a greater understanding of how average Americans existed, many felt, something perhaps less exciting than the revolutionary ideas of the Founding Fathers but equally valuable as a history lesson. "Our colonial ancestors were like us in most ways—working, playing, and living in a country full of promise," noted Stephanie Slahor of California State College's School of Education, offering a number of activities that contemporary families could do to better understand and appreciate the formers' normal lives. Making jerky (dried meat), baking bread, churning butter, sewing a doll's dress, or weaving a blanket were all opportunities to "try colonial living in your home," Slahor advised. [168]

Such tips were reflective of the shift that had taken place in the trajectory of the Bicentennial. Washington was now moving in the right direction after years of mismanagement, but Americans had already come to the conclusion that they were better equipped to celebrate the event in their own, more localized ways. "The major planning has been wrested from the hands of big government and entrusted to the powers of the people," an editor for the Los Angeles *Sunday Herald-Examiner* observed, thinking that this was "an historically valid way to proceed since it's precisely how it all started a couple of hundred years ago."[169]

Looking back, the shift was quite a remarkable one. Until relatively recently, it had been assumed that there would be a whopping event in Philadelphia, Boston, or Washington, DC, with the rest of the country acting more or less as spectators. For many reasons, that was not the way that plans proceeded, however, leaving a kind of vacuum that all could feel. Those cities were the geographic origins of the American Revolution, after all, making it understandable why that model had dominated the conversation. The federal government's failure to bring forth something worthy of the occasion, however, had led to the recognition that there had to be a better path lest the "once-in-a-lifetime" opportunity be missed. "The whole concept has been decentralized from Washington to the local communities where it belongs," the editorial wisely concluded.[170]

Decentralization of the Bicentennial hardly meant that what was termed the "Colonial Corridor" would be vacant in 1975 and 1976, however. Since the event had been first proposed, planners in New England had been worried about the stream of traffic that would arrive those two years, creating havoc across the area. This had not changed; in fact, such fears had intensified due to the findings of a survey conducted by the Bicentennial Council of the Thirteen Original States. Somewhere between 550 million and 876 million visits would be made to the Colonial Corridor in 1976 alone, according to the research, and the area was not at all equipped to handle that number of tourists and cars.[171]

Open to suggestions regarding how to address a traffic jam of epic proportions, that council was heeding advice from the

Washington Center for Metropolitan Studies, which had recently produced a report on the issue. Recommendations included opening a travel center to offer assistance to visitors; setting up a toll-free telephone number providing details on sites and events; airing bulletins on radio and television delivering real-time travel information; training more Bicentennial guides; and improving and expanding transportation systems. The biggest problem appeared to be the lack of coordination among officials in the many communities located along the corridor, however, as they were focused on their individual sites. Unless steps were taken, "local embarrassment and loss of revenues can be very high," the report soberly warned.[172]

A Groundswell of Grass Roots Activity

Since coming into office in August 1974, President Ford had been largely quiet about the Bicentennial, his only official announcement being the appointments of Marjorie Lynch as deputy administrator of the ARBA and a number of appointments to its board.[173] The media made much of the fact that Ford had selected "a woman born in England," as the *New York Times* put it, to the post. (Lynch had come to the United States in 1945 as a war bride.) "I wanted a woman in the No. 2 job," Warner said after Lynch was appointed deputy administrator, "and the fact that she is an immigrant is beautiful." (Lynch, meanwhile, said she never felt like an immigrant.) Lynch, who was a Republican and had deep experience in governmental affairs, specifically in the area of funding, would handle most of the day-to-day managerial tasks while Warner was on the road promoting the Bicentennial and raising money.[174]

With Warner, the ARBA was rather suddenly getting good reviews. Despite all the false starts and missteps, there was "a groundswell of grass roots activity that adds up to a prideful national celebration," UPI senior editor Frederick M. Winship wrote in November 1974. Particularly notable was an ARBA program in which 1,659 villages, towns, and cities had to date been designated a "Bicentennial Community," which allowed them to fly official flags and display official insignia. As important, those communities were eligible for state-awarded funds drawn from the ARBA's $8 million budget.[175]

It wasn't intentional, of course, but Warner felt that his predecessors' failure to put together a national Bicentennial exposition or world's fair in a big East Coast city had been a blessing in disguise. Such a thing would have diverted attention from the thousands of local events that were already taking place across the country and served as "the heart of the celebration," he maintained. Indeed, Warner had just returned to Washington from the opening of an agricultural museum in Stuttgart, Arkansas, and a mining museum in the aptly named Centennial, Wyoming. Such towns had absolutely no connection to the American Revolution, but that was no deterrent to the communities wanting to be somehow involved in the Bicentennial—a very good sign.[176]

During its tenure, the ARBC had defined three themes that local communities should try to adhere in their own celebrations: "Heritage '76" (history); "Open House USA" (education); and "Horizon '76" (participation). While those themes had shifted somewhat under the direction of the ARBA toward more of a festival approach, most local events did indeed fall within the parameters of the themes. Historical restorations, performing arts events (especially opera and choral works), and civic improvements were the most common activities, and reenactments were proving to be popular as well. Green Mountain Boys would capture Fort Ticonderoga, New York, on May 10, 1975, as the original ones did two hundred years earlier, and General Richard Montgomery's march from Rhinebeck, New York, to Quebec would be repeated (this time by car).[177]

Museums found creative ways to connect their respective collections to the Bicentennial.

Some events, such as the "Chilimpiad" (a chili contest in Texas), seemed to stray a bit from the three recommended Bicentennial themes, but no one seemed to mind. Managers of the birthplaces of John Adam and John Quincy Adams in Quincy, Massachusetts, had decided to put central heating in the old houses as their Bicentennial effort, historically questionable but a sensible choice that would make winter visitors to the sites no doubt quite happy.[178]

No one could say for sure, of course, but some were forecasting that more than half of America's population of 200 million would somehow participate in Bicentennial-related activity. "Americans are embarked on an unprecedented wingding that underscores the nation's unity in diversity," Winship wrote, labeling the Bicentennial as "a series of sideshows without a main event." Best of all, perhaps, some communities were finding interesting ways to take part without having to spend a lot of money. Four hundred volunteers (aged nine to seventy-nine) in South Bend, Indiana, for example, painted the city's fireplugs to look like American Revolutionary War soldiers. Volunteers in Desha County, Arkansas, cleaned up a World War II–era Japanese detention camp cemetery, an excellent way to recognize shameful incidents in American history.[179]

Some communities, however, were dipping deep into their budgets. Officials in Sacramento, California, for example, were spending $700,000 ($4.5 million in today's money) on a monument commemorating the debut trip of the Pony Express to the state's capital. That was peanuts compared to what the Metropolitan Museum of Art in New York was shelling out, however. The museum (with considerable help from the federal government) was spending $11.9 million to create an American Bicentennial

Wing to hold the world's largest collection of American decorative arts. (The "Bicentennial" was later dropped.) Washington, DC, had finally decided on a worthy and costly project: a forty-five-acre Constitution Garden on the Mall. Nearby in Alexandria, Virginia, the 1839 Lyceum Building was restored as the George Washington Bicentennial Center and Museum featuring life in eighteenth-century Virginia.[180]

While African Americans and Native Americans had each been underrepresented in Bicentennial planning, there would be some recognition of their respective cultural contributions. An exhibition

The National Visitor Center in Union Station, Washington, DC, under construction in 1976.

of four hundred works depicting "The Black in America History" was being put together in Cleveland, and Jackson (Mississippi) State College planned to sponsor a Phyllis Wheatley Poetry Festival. (Wheatley, a slave, was recognized as the first Black person in the

United States to publish a book of poems.) The Navajo Nation was organizing an arts and dance exposition in Window Rocks, Arizona, for 1976, and the Stockbridge-Munsee Indians were constructing a museum and library on their Wisconsin reservation. Another Native American project in the works was the re-creation of a pioneer Creek home in Okmulgee, Oklahoma.[181]

As all these projects took shape, the ARBA was busy making its own plans but finding it was well short of the money to complete all of them. Roughly $50 million in additional funds was required, it estimated, and there was little chance that it was going to come from the federal government. Congress had bumped up its annual contribution to $10 million, but that money went toward administrative costs, grants to states, and planning and development. Warner stepped up his corporate sponsorship efforts, trying to leverage partnerships made with IBM, J.C. Penney, American Express, and a few others. J.C. Penny was paying the $2 million bill for every high school band and choral group in the country to receive a set of scores of American music, while American Express had chipped in $120,000 to the U.S. Park Service to refurbish the Statue of Liberty.[182]

Some critics were complaining that the Bicentennial had already become overly commercial, prompting Warner to reply that involvement from the private sector was essential if the American people were going to have something of which they would be proud. State and local groups were following suit; Boston planners had received $1 million from Salada Tea, John Hancock Insurance, and other companies, and Ethan Allen furniture had contributed $100,000 for a mobile exhibit in Vermont. In Mississippi, Masonite Corporation was financing a conservation program targeted to elementary school students, and Pennsylvania

Bell Telephone was picking up the tab for a series of pageants to be held at Carpenter's Hall in Philadelphia. (The First Continental Congress met there for six weeks in the fall of 1774.)[183]

Now four months into his job and seeing Warner make real progress in getting Americans excited about the Bicentennial, the president began to take a more active role in its proceedings. Ford seemed particularly interested in the American Freedom Train, making a December 1974 appearance at the Alexandria, Virginia railroad station to launch that project. The train was "one of the focal points of our bicentennial celebration," he told a crowd of five hundred (mostly schoolchildren on field trips and staff members). About one hundred demonstrators for Rifkin's People's Bicentennial Commission were there as well, voicing their protest against anything smacking of what they saw as jingoistic pageantry.[184]

Ford was undeterred by the heckling ("Jobs, not circus," they chanted), however, saying that he viewed the Bicentennial as "a rebirth" of the country and "a rediscovery of our strength and our potential." The president used the occasion to present George Washington's copy of the Constitution to Donald Kendall, CEO of Pepsi-Cola; that company was one of five major sponsors of the American Freedom Train. John Warner was there, keeping his word that the ARBA would find corporate partners to help pay for larger Bicentennial projects. The train, which had begun to tour the country in July 1974, was nicknamed "The Preamble Express" for what it carried on board. "Let us reaffirm our faith in the American spirit," Ford proclaimed, borrowing the kind of language that his predecessor had used in promoting the Bicentennial.[185] The nation's two hundredth birthday party had begun, but the celebration was about to take some unpredictable twists and turns.

An enormous, spontaneous, democratic, colorful and confusing explosion of Bicentennial energy is shaping up.

—Margot Hornblower, *Washington Post*, February 1975

3.

A Richly Diverse Mosaic

"Bicentennial Fever Spreads Across U.S," read a front-page headline in the *Washington Post* in February 1975 as reports from across the nation came in. A small museum in Sitka, Alaska (population 3,370), was organizing an exhibit on life of Tlingit Indians in 1776, while the Florida Bicentennial Commission had carved out a trail designating one hundred historic sites from St. Augustine to the Kennedy Space Center. Officials in Greensburg, Louisiana, were turning an old jail into a museum, and the postal service of Macomb Township, Michigan, had decided to paint the area's mailboxes red, white, and blue. "With the Bicentennial year only 10 months away, the ferment of activity is swinging into full gear," the article continued, with Americans "writing books, mounting exhibits, restoring houses, re-enacting battles, organizing conferences, planting trees, and planning festivals and fireworks, all in honor of the nation's 200th anniversary in 1976."[186]

Bicentennial fever had taken almost a decade to develop, but many Americans were happy to have a case of it. For years, plans for the Bicentennial had remained in limbo, with one idea after another failing to materialize due to dissension, cost, or lack of inertia. While it appeared that the event was finally coming together as a collection of thousands of local celebrations rather than a single, huge one, not all Americans were pleased to see its approach. As much as anything else, in fact, the Bicentennial in 1975 would be defined by minorities' strong feelings that they were being treated as less than equal partners in its planning, something entirely consistent with the discrimination that they had always faced.

A Rare and Important Opportunity

Confronting that situation head-on, the ARBA decided to sponsor a three-day conference in January 1975 specifically to address what was described as "minority involvement." More than two hundred congressmen, businesspeople, heads of nonprofits, and federal officials showed up in Washington to discuss the issue, which had simmered since the early stages of planning for the Bicentennial. Some were hopeful that progress would be made while others remained skeptical. "This is another talkathon," said Vincent DeForest, who had cofounded with his brother the Afro-American Bicentennial Corporation, seeing no reason why the ARBA would decide to change its policies. Charles Wesley, a Black historian and author, was more optimistic, thinking that the gathering had value. "Over 5,000 blacks were involved in the American Revolution," he noted, hopeful that the ARBA would finally put into practice the principles of the Founding Fathers.[187]

For people of color, 1975 appeared to be a tipping point in terms of their stance toward the Bicentennial. As at the January

ARBA conference, African Americans were divided on whether they should as Americans celebrate the Bicentennial, use it to illustrate their contribution to the nation's history, or exploit it to demonstrate their past and present oppression. For Gloria C. Oden of *Essence* magazine, it was a combination of all three sentiments. "The Bicentennial presents a rare and important opportunity for the Black community to impress upon itself and its white counterpart the sacrifices we have endured in making this nation rich and prosperous," she wrote, of the mind that the event "must reflect the total Black American experience." Black history was "as replete with drama as any other," she stated, urging Hollywood in particular to recognize that fact when making movies about African American culture versus the "blaxploitation" films they were currently making.[188]

Academics working in the area of Afro-American studies recognized that the Bicentennial was a propitious moment to revise and expand Black history and raise the profile of the field. Bibliographies documenting the significant body of work completed to date in the area were published, one of them in early 1975 in the *Negro History Bulletin*. Delores C. Leffall of the Moorland-Spingarn Research Center at Howard University selected books and articles that covered a wide range of topics relating to African American culture, including general history, employment, politics, education, housing, psychology, religion, and local historic sites and monuments. More colleges and high schools were already offering classes or starting departments in Afro-American studies, and Black scholars saw the Bicentennial as a means of accelerating the field's growth.[189]

For journalists of the country's eleven major Black newspapers (the *Atlanta Daily World*, *Baltimore Afro-American*, *Chicago*

Defender, *Cleveland Call and Post*, *Louisville Defender*, *Los Angeles Sentinel*, *Michigan Chronicle*, *New York Amsterdam News*, *Norfolk Journal and Guide*, *Philadelphia Tribune*, and *Pittsburgh Courier*), the Bicentennial was an ideal opportunity to point out the contradictions between America's proud claims of democracy and equality and the actual African American experience. From the spring of 1975 right up to July 4, 1976, dozens of articles appeared in the Black press addressing the incongruities attached to the celebration of an event that, more than anything else, extolled the noble values of freedom and liberty.

For syndicated columnist William L. Patterson, for example, the Bicentennial was that of "a racist state"; for White Americans, the event served as "a moral crisis for which they have neither answers nor remedy." The myth of White superiority still shaped the workings of politics, economics, and education, Patterson pointed out, thinking that "the Bicentennial celebration poses vital questions" regarding how Americans should address the wide gap between ideology and reality, particularly with regard to employment.[190] Dick Gregory, the comedian turned activist, believed the United States should "start off the Bicentennial by using $150 million to build up this nation and see to it that there are jobs for everyone."[191]

Contradictorily, perhaps, the Black press was also eager to provide readers with ways in which African Americans were participating in the Bicentennial and demonstrating their prominent role in the nation's history. A Ford Motor Company–sponsored exhibit called Living Legends in Black, for example, was in the making, the *Atlanta Daily World* reported. The two hundred black-and-white photographs of contemporary African Americans and their achievements taken by J. Edward Bailey III would be in shown in Washington, DC, and then in Detroit and other cities.[192]

More of those kinds of exhibitions were needed, according to a group calling itself the Association for the Study of Afro-American Life and History. The organization held a National Bicentennial Heritage Conference in April 1975 in Washington to come up with ways to "encourage broad participation by Blacks in the Bicentennial effort," as its executive director stated. Heads of national organizations, state and local Bicentennial agencies, and the media were all invited to attend.[193]

Those attendees were no doubt pleased to see African Americans' significant representation in the American Freedom Train. Blacks were featured "in every facet of American history throughout its twelve-car exhibit," noted the *Atlanta Daily World*, taking special note of Car 10. It was in that car, named "The Conflict and Resolution," where visitors could see and hear films of African Americans marching in protest and an excerpt of Dr. Martin Luther King's "I Have a Dream" speech. There was a life-size replica of King's pulpit as well (the original remained in Ebenezer Baptist Church in Atlanta). While many were happy to see such representations of the civil rights movement in Car 10, one had to wonder how there was "resolution" to the "conflict."[194]

Other American Americans viewed the Bicentennial as a generally inclusive event. "There is a place for everyone in the upcoming bicentennial celebration," wrote Darcelle Kanoyton for the *Michigan Chronicle*, thinking that "the role of Black people in that history will be no exception." Kanoyton was based in Detroit, where African Americans were more involved in local planning than most other places. (Detroit would be celebrating its 275th birthday in 1976.) A few notable Bicentennial projects addressing African American culture were in progress or being discussed, including an exhibit on Black life in the colonial era at the Afro-American Museum of Detroit, a Black jazz festival, and the reconstruction of the Woodward East area.[195]

Whereas some African Americans were strongly opposed to the Bicentennial because of its hypocrisy and others saw it as predominantly egalitarian, there was a contingent who had ambivalent feelings toward the event. As with the world wars, the Bicentennial posed a dilemma of sorts for African Americans whose identities were naturally rooted in both nation and race. During World War II, this double or dual identity had been well established, particularly by Swedish economist Gunnar Myrdal's *An American Dilemma: The Negro Problem and Modern Democracy*. Three decades later, the dilemma again surfaced due to the Bicentennial, well-evidenced by the good question James P. Murray posed in the New York Amsterdam News in June 1975: "How do we celebrate?"[196]

Expectedly, given its usually moderate position, the NAACP was in this middle ground between objection to and support for the Bicentennial. More than anything else, the NAACP urged that Blacks be recognized for their role in American history from the Revolution (notably that of Crispus Attucks, the first American to die in the war) right up to recent times (notably that of Martin Luther King Jr.). Chapters of the NAACP in every state in the country should make sure that African Americans at minimum "ride shotgun," said William Powell, head of publicity for the Pennsylvania branch, advocating that minority businesses be involved in local projects.[197]

Elizabet Hood, writing for the *Michigan Chronicle*, conceded that the 200th anniversary of the signing of the Declaration of Independence sounded like "a real gig" while at the same time acknowledged that "many Blacks are hesitating to accept the invitation to celebrate the bicentennial." Why were a good number of

African Americans choosing not to attend the party? "The 'shot that was heard around the world' on the 18th of April in '75 did not ring for them," Hood noted, thinking like some others that the millions of dollars being spent on the Bicentennial could be put to much more productive uses. Still, "the bicentennial can be a time for consciousness-raising and for charting a future firmly rooted in the realities of the Black Experience," Hood felt, an excellent way to interpret the event.[198]

A Bicentennial Declaration

Native Americans too were finding ways to make the Bicentennial meaningful. Like the DeForests, who had decided to take matters in their own hands through their Afro-American Bicentennial Corporation rather than wait for the ARBC to embrace diversity, some Native Americans were acting independently. With funding from the Mississippi Bicentennial Commission, for example, Choctaw high school students in central Mississippi were documenting their culture while it still existed. (Older people were dying off and younger people were increasingly assimilating.) The students were interviewing craftspeople, learning traditional music and dance, and documenting traditional Choctaw food and clothing as well as its folklore. The teenagers documented their findings in their own quarterly magazine, *Nanih Waiya*, and integrating them within a history course taught at their school.[199]

Minority groups' efforts to make the Bicentennial their own reflected the plasticity of American identity and how the event was meaning different things to different people. As interesting as those efforts were, they comprised a small fraction of the

Log cabins served as a tangible reminder of the nation's pioneer past.

total effort being expended toward the nation's two hundredth birthday. Many agencies of the federal government were involved, and there were commissions in not just all fifty states but the District of Columbia, Puerto Rico, Guam, and American Samoa. Some 2,400 communities in the United States had programs in place, as did ten Indian reservations and twenty-two foreign countries. Thousands of corporations, unions, schools, religious groups, and other organizations were sponsoring Bicentennial projects, all of this making it understandable why the ARBA had labeled the event "a richly diverse mosaic" of community-based celebrations. The students, staff, and parents of Park Orchard Elementary School in Kent, Washington, built by hand a whole Indian village along with two log cabins and a log barn.[200]

It was safe to say that big corporations' interest in the Bicentennial was primarily to align themselves with America itself, as the event was the most nationalistic thing to come along

Retailers like this supermarket were eager to tie in to the Bicentennial.

since the World War II war bond campaign. Generating goodwill among the public was thus behind corporate sponsorships, but the publicity to be gained was the larger goal. Banks, retailers, insurance companies, and manufacturers of all kinds of products were either partnering with the government at the federal, state, or local level or else pursuing projects of their own to retain control. Restoring a historic district, building a park, or putting up a monument were common ways for companies to tie in to the Bicentennial.

Certain kinds of businesses were naturally benefiting from Bicentennial fever. Not surprisingly, antique dealers, particularly those specializing in colonial (pre-1776) Americana, were very excited about the opportunities that the event was already bringing. Those who knew their history were familiar with the fact that it had been the 1876 Centennial that had stirred Americans to start collecting important eighteenth-century furniture, furnishings, paintings, and decorative arts, the beginnings of some of the great antique collections in the country. The Bicentennial would only add to Americans' accelerating interest in their history, dealers believed, as the 1970s were already turning out to be a decade heavily defined by a longing for times that seemed simpler and more authentic. "Americans have a growing penchant for their past and an expanding appreciation for ingenuity and quality of bygone American craftmanship," Marilyn Hoffman of the *Christian Science Monitor* observed after going to the Armory antique show in New York.[201]

Opportunity also knocked for contemporary crafters as the Bicentennial approached. "The market for American handcrafts is flourishing, especially with the Bicentennial coming up," noted Margaret Daly in *Better Homes and Gardens*, thinking "there couldn't be a better time" to sell one's work. Every state in the union was planning to have some kind of craft show or fair in 1975 or 1976, an excellent setting to show handmade pottery, stitchery, woodwork, oils, or other artistic creations. The field was highly competitive, Daly warned hobbyists who aspired to become pros, advising them to approach their work as a business rather than as a fun pastime if one's goal was to make money.[202]

Whether it was a large corporation or a knitter of teapot cozies, making money was often the driving force to literally capitalize on the major and still growing interest in the Bicentennial. Some members of the ARBA advisory council (including James Michener, author of the recently published novel *Bicentennial*) were concerned that commercial interests were overwhelming the significance of the event. The lack of a single theme linking the thousands of events together was said to have contributed to this; another advisory council member, the African American poet Maya

Angelou, urged the group to "think of something unifying." Still, it was inevitable that marketing would heavily infiltrate the event regardless of its form, as it was too big of an opportunity to reach a mass audience to go ignored by corporate America.[203]

In fact, one could argue that there was a single unifying theme of the Bicentennial: Americans from all walks of life making the event meaningful by personalizing it in some way. In March 1975, the Schroeder family of Valparaiso, Indiana, was reading American history together and planned to continue doing so until July 4, 1976. Burton and Burnie Burkman, brothers in Sioux Falls, South Dakota, had begun to plant, cultivate, and harvest crops on their fifty-acre farm "pioneer-style," i.e., using horses rather than machinery. John Wallace of Northport, New York, was making an exact replica of the kite used by Benjamin Franklin in his lightning experiment, while Indiana prison inmate Joe Kunz was carving by hand a chess set featuring George and Martha Washington as a king and queen. (King George III and his wife, Charlotte, served as the opposing side's king and queen.)[204]

The list of what Clayton Jones of the *Christian Science Monitor* called "do-it-yourself Bicentennial plans" went on and on. Mitsugi Ohno, a physics instructor at Kansas State University, was making a five-foot replica of the U.S. Capitol building in red, white, and blue glass (a three-year project), while Patricia Paden of Needham, Massachusetts, was planting geraniums in those same three colors. (Thomas Jefferson reportedly grew the first scarlet geraniums in America.) Finally, the Nesbitt family of Oswego, New York, was preparing to retrace the steps that their great-great-great-great-great grandfather took during the Battle of Lake Ontario in the War of 1812 (which was, of course, also against the British).[205]

Given such stories, a do-it-yourself Bicentennial seemed a fitting way to celebrate the event in a society so focused on the individual or self. As well, making the Bicentennial one's own was a reaction to what many Americans felt was its overcommercialism and top-heaviness in terms of government programming. In a sense, then, one could say that individuals were rebelling against a dictatorial regime, a fitting tribute to the American Revolution.[206]

One man, however, was thinking much bigger and using his considerable resources to try to convince others to adopt his rather radical views. John D. Rockefeller III, the businessman and philanthropist, had recently authored a book called *The Second American Revolution* in which he argued that "this is the time for the people to lead the government rather than vice versa."[207] Taking a cue from the Founding Fathers, Rockefeller had created a document titled "A Bicentennial Declaration," whose text was published in March 1975 issues of *Time* and *Newsweek*. The "Declaration" was also scheduled to run in about forty newspapers across the country, and the three major television networks and their affiliates planned to broadcast the text. In a nutshell, Rockefeller believed that twentieth-century Americans needed to recommit to the ideals put forth two hundred years earlier, thinking that we had lost our way in living up to the bold vision expressed in the Declaration of Independence.[208]

Others felt that the Bicentennial had simply come at a bad time in American history. It was unfortunate that the event hadn't come along a decade ago, when the United States was at the peak of its powers or a decade hence, when solutions to the problems of the day had likely been found. It was true that the country had yet to fully recover from the early 1970s recession, that there had recently been major political upheaval, and that the energy crisis had made Americans question their oil-dependent way of life. William H. Stringer, however, felt it was a perfect time to celebrate the nation's Bicentennial, as the event reminded Americans how troubles and disasters of the past had been conquered. We should welcome these days which "try men's souls," Stringer argued, as they made us appreciate how resilient a society we really were. (Stringer was now, it should be mentioned, a senior editor in the ARBA press office.)[209]

America on Parade

Addressing some of American's problems was a major component of the American Issues Forum, which would kick off in September 1975 and run through May 1976. One issue each month would be discussed, with the media, schools, labor unions, churches, service clubs, and politicians all welcome to make their voices heard. It was CBS news anchor Walter Cronkite who had first proposed the idea, and now the NEH was handling the logistics. Some of the issues were: How has America fared as a "nation of immigrants"? To what goals do we "pledge our allegiance"? Do we truly believe there are "certain alienable rights," as mentioned in the Constitution? Have the "separation of powers" been effective? Is the United States the "most productive" nation on earth, as widely claimed?[210]

These were all good questions and worthy of debate to acknowledge the concerns of some that the Bicentennial should be an opportunity for Americans to take a hard look at the nation's past in order to chart a course for the future. Still, there had to be some more pleasurable experiences, especially if they somehow related to life in colonial America. That could be definitely seen at the gala luncheon at the opening of Boston's Museum of Fine Arts Bicentennial exhibition, *Paul Revere's Boston*. Guests munched on authentic eighteenth-century New England dishes such as Liberty Tree Turkey, Independent Asparagus, and Plymouth Pâté while viewing period paintings, silver, furniture, prints, documents, and decorative arts and listening to a fiddler play English and Irish tunes of the 1770s. The event was a re-creation of a luncheon served by Mrs. John Hancock, who was known in her day as an especially gracious host.[211]

Many new trees were planted in the United States for the Bicentennial, including these in Constitution Gardens.

A re-creation of George Washington's inauguration day parade in Washington, DC.

President Ford missed the lunch but was in Boston two days later promoting the Bicentennial and the Republican's pro–big business, anti–big government platform. Ford made speeches at the Old North Church in Boston and in Concord, New Hampshire, which politicos recognized as the beginning of his reelection campaign. "As we launch this Bicentennial celebration, we Americans must remind ourselves of the eternal truth by which we live," he said at the site where two hundred years earlier two lanterns shone in the church steeple, sending Paul Revere on his ride to warn that the Redcoats were coming.[212] That ride would be repeated by one Dino De Carlo, a sixty-one-year-old contractor, complete with Reverian breeches, waistcoat, and peruke (wig).[213]

A shelf of new books documenting Revere's ride and many other elements of the American Revolution were not surprisingly being published. In addition to a handful of recently published biographies of famous figures (Aaron Burr, Thomas Jefferson, George Washington, Benjamin Franklin, Thomas Paine, John

Marshall), there were studies of lesser-known characters such as Edmund Randolph (Washington's most trusted advisor, later accused of treason) and painter/patriot John Trumbull.[214]

Alongside these biographies were a number of books that parsed details of the American Revolution, so many in fact that they comprised a mini-literary genre all their own. These included Dumas Malone's *The Story of the Declaration of Independence*; Franklin Folsom's *Give Me Liberty*; Murray N. Rothbard's *Conceived in Liberty*; Samuel Rezneck's *Unrecognized Patriots*; Robert Ewell Greene's *Black Defenders of America*; Duncan J. MacLeod's *Slavery, Race and the American Revolution*; Sidney Kaplan's *The Black Presence in the Era of the American Revolution*; Daniel Sisson's *The American Revolution of 1800*; Ralph Ketcham's *From Colony to Country: The Revolution in American Thought 1750–1820*; and Dave Richard Palmer's *The Way of the Fox* (the fox being military strategist General George Washington).[215]

Libraries across the country were not surprisingly playing an active role in Bicentennial programs, no more so than the Boston Public Library. That institution kicked off a twenty-month series on "Literary Boston" with featured readings, discussions, and lectures by notable writers who happened to live in the area. Archibald MacLeish read a specially commissioned poem, while other important literary figures, including Howard Mumford Jones, gave talks to go along with the library's rather awkwardly named exhibit, *Boston: A State of Mind, a 300-Year Dialogue Between Author and Audience*. In New York City, the Brooklyn Public Library curated a Bicentennial exhibit featuring what was described as "contemporary crafts with origins in colonial America." Rather than scour for actual eighteenth-century works, in other words, the library had local Brooklyn artists create stained glass, pottery, needlepoints, and other crafts in the style of the period, an interesting approach that drew on direct community involvement.[216]

Public libraries' Bicentennial initiatives were part of a concerted effort to make the nation's history accessible to a wide audience. Notable scholars with a more populist bent were invited by the media to reflect on the American idea and experience from a historical perspective. *Time*, for example, asked leading American historian Daniel J. Boorstin to write a "Bicentennial Essay" for the magazine in June 1975, giving a large audience a tutorial in the nation's founding. In his essay (Boorstin also served as an adviser to *Time* on the series), he reminded readers that our nation was a "byproduct," i.e., that the goal of the Revolutionary War was independence rather than nationhood.[217]

Other Bicentennial Essays, which ran through early 1976, focused on the presidency, work, child rearing, science, communications, art, food, healthcare, and law. *Time*, which was ubiquitous before the advent of cable news in the 1980s, had already had a Bicentennial hit with its special July 4, 1976 issue. That issue (featuring Thomas Jefferson on the cover) was especially popular with schools and organizations, particularly because it could be purchased at bulk rates. The first run of 5.4 million copies nearly sold out in three weeks, compelling the publisher to order a second printing (the first time in the magazine's history).[218]

There was no more popular celebration of the Bicentennial than the ones held at Disney World and Disneyland, however. Every day between July 1975 and September 1976, Disney presented "America on Parade" to visitors, a spectacle that an estimated 25 million visitors would see. (My future wife, then two years old, was one of them.) Fifty floats and 150 characters went down Main

Street, U.S.A., in each park's parade to the backdrop of marching bands. The eight- to ten-foot characters were not just drawn from Disney's universe of entertainment but also included what was described as the "People of America." Sailors to the New World, colonial soldiers, Western frontiersmen, and Tom Sawyer and his friends were such "people," although a flag-bearing Mickey Mouse, Goofy, and Donald Duck naturally led the parade.[219]

Cleverly, Disney (the company rather than the man, who had died in 1966) featured a different state each week in "America on Parade" (in order of joining the Union). The parade ran twice each day (free with admission), and Disney also waived the usual fee for its *Hall of Presidents* in the CircleVision 360 Theater. Many visitors were eager to see the animatronic Abraham Lincoln and other presidents at Disney World, but it was the park's new rides—the Space Mountain roller coaster, the People-Mover, and revamped Mission to Mars—that really drew the crowds.[220]

The federal government could not resist popularizing the Bicentennial. New coins were designed and minted for the anniversary and, judging by the number planned to be produced (300 million Eisenhower dollars, 550 million Kennedy half dollars, and 1.6 billion Washington quarters), were fully intended to be used rather than just become collectors' items. The front sides of the coins remained the same except for a new date range (1776–1976), while their reverse sides all featured new images—the Liberty Bell and a cratered moon for the dollar; Independence Hall for the half dollar; and a colonial drummer boy for the quarter.[221]

Not to be left out, the U.S. Postal Service soon announced that it would release a sheet of fifty stamps to honor the all the states for the Bicentennial. Each stamp would bear the respective state flag, with the sheet arranged in order of admittance to the Union.

In addition to that issue, the USPS planned to release a sheet of thirty-two stamps honoring the Declaration of Independence; each of the stamps would include a small portion of the document. Oddly, perhaps, the American Philatelic Society was not supporting either of these issues; sheets of thirty-two and especially fifty stamps were much too large for their liking.[222]

In the Midst of American Society

While the Bicentennial took on ever-greater proportions on the national scene, African Americans continued to discuss if and how they should approach the event. Charles E. Price of the *Atlanta Daily World* made the case that the "Bicentennial celebration is for us, too," feeling Blacks had not only the right to participate but also the duty. Price believed those arguing that people of color should abstain from the event because of the ugly history of racism were missing the point; the Bicentennial was about the Revolution, which had planted the seeds for a nation that had endured for two centuries. Many revolutions didn't last two years, much less two centuries, Price correctly pointed out, feeling that all Americans were obligated to respect this remarkable achievement despite the nation's many flaws.[223]

Of course, the fact that many of the signers of the Declaration of Independence owned slaves complicated matters for those African Americans negotiating their participation in the Bicentennial. How was it possible for the same people who endorsed the revolutionary idea that "all men are created free and equal" to personally sanction the possession of another human being? Why did the right to "life, liberty and the pursuit of happiness" apply only to certain individuals? Black historian John Hope Franklin addressed such questions in an article titled "The Moral Legacy of the Founding Fathers" that was published in the Summer 1975 issue of the *University of Chicago Magazine*. In short, Franklin had no doubts that the Founding Fathers acted heroically, but he also saw them as "frail, fallible human beings," as all of us were.[224]

Ebony magazine, along with *Jet*, its sibling publication, were approaching the Bicentennial by featuring articles on African Americans who had made or were making a significant contribution to the building of the nation. For its special Bicentennial issue in August 1975, *Ebony* showed how "long before the wave of European immigration began, black labor was the backbone of the American economy," and how "black brainpower" was responsible for a variety of inventions and innovations. Historians, religious leaders, civil rights activists, and a few of the magazine's editors all contributed articles to the issue.[225]

The positions that contributors to the *Ebony* issue took toward Black participation in the Bicentennial were expectedly mixed. Scholar and social historian Lerone Bennet Jr. urged African Americans to not join in, thinking the event called for "mourning and struggle, not celebration." Vernon Jordan, national director of the Urban League, was highly skeptical about the direction the Bicentennial was taking, thinking middle-aged men marching around in three-cornered hats was a rather silly way to go about what could be a meaningful event. Writing for the *Cleveland Call and Post*, the Reverend Arthur Zebbs of Columbus, Ohio, saw no reason for the Bicentennial unless the true story of America was told, exposing all of its lies and myths with regard to race. Zebbs didn't see that happening, but he wasn't overly upset about it.

"I'd rather listen to Aretha Franklin and Marvin Gaye, anyway," he remarked.[226]

Black journalists and notable figures had platforms to express their views on the stance that African Americans should take for the Bicentennial, but how did the "man or woman on the street" feel about it? An editor of the *Pittsburgh Courier* asked that very question and sent a reporter to learn some answers. The newspaper discovered that "most brothers and sisters 'don't give a damn'" about the Bicentennial, the editor wrote, the general feeling being that Blacks were vastly underrepresented in the programs so far presented. One woman interviewed was opting out of all things Bicentennial simply because both the government and public education system expressed little interest in the lives of minorities as a whole, a fair assessment circa 1975.[227]

It was exactly those two sentiments that led the ARBA to urge states to include minorities, women, and young people in any Bicentennial plans that used federal money. Representative Patricia Schroeder (D-CO and chair of the House census and population subcommittee) had proposed that such activities be required on a quota basis, but the ARBA passed on that recommendation. Matching grants of $40,000 were going to each of the fifty states and U.S. territories, but they carried a stipulation that the funds should be targeted to programs involving "women, youth, and racial and ethnic groups."[228]

Under intensified political pressure to be more inclusive, the ARBA in August 1975 established an advisory committee dedicated to ethnic and racial participation in the Bicentennial. The committee consisted of representatives from a startling number of groups, including (in no particular order) Pacific Islanders, Italians, British, Native Americans, Chinese, Greeks, Hispanics,

African Americans, Irish, Poles, Swedes, Ukrainians, Japanese, and Czechoslovakians. "I am deeply appreciative of the willingness of these Americans to serve on the committee to help us ensure full participation by all our people in the Bicentennial," John Warner said in announcing the appointments.[229]

With that significant decision, African American, Native American, and White ethnic groups stepped up their Bicentennial plans or were at least urged to do so by state or local commission leaders. Stanley Balzekas Jr., chair of the ethnic subcommittee of the Chicago Bicentennial Committee, for example, asked his fellow ethnic Chicagoans to share their unique heritages with the larger community. Balzekas was working with individual volunteers and organizations to hold a three-day celebration for various ethnic groups as well as a citywide Bicentennial festival.[230]

American Jews were also finding ways to infuse the Bicentennial with meaning that spoke to their cultural identity. The New York City–based Jewish Welfare Board Lecture Bureau made available some eighty-five lecturers and performers who were equipped to present programs on Jewish aspects of the American Revolution and could be booked in local communities. The lectures were far-ranging, with titles including "Contributions of Jews and Judaism to America," "Women in American Jewish History," and "Colonial Jewry." Performances, meanwhile, included *The Magnificent Melting Pot*, *L'Chaim America*, and *Two Hundred Years of the Jewish Experience in America*. Jews had played an important role in the history of the nation, the lectures and performances collectively showed, with the Bicentennial serving as an ideal opportunity to tell Americans just that.[231]

The circumstances were much different, of course, but more moderate African Americans also believed the Bicentennial represented a rare chance that shouldn't be missed. "There will never be a better time to offer proof to the civilized world the positive achievements and contributions Black Americans have given in the building of this nation," wrote James A. Cobb in a letter to the editor of the *Michigan Chronicle*. Historians had failed in this regard, Cobb correctly argued, making it fellow African Americans' job to get their story right during the Bicentennial. The federal government had also failed in ensuring their promises be kept, more reason to point that out while much of the country was listening. "We must take advantage of every opportunity to remind white America that we have earned our places not on the sidelines but in the midst of American society," Cobb concluded his letter.[232]

The opening of *The Black Presence in the Era of the American Revolution, 1700–1800* would help achieve that worthy goal. The exhibit was crisscrossing the country via the Smithsonian Institution Traveling Service, taking occupancy in a museum or historical society in a major city for about a month before moving on to another. Restoring historic facts to the national memory was a key aim of the show, with forty panels telling the story of Blacks in the eighteenth century. Rather than just slaves, Black Americans were through that century "soldier and sailor, founder of the Black church, fighter for equality organizer of schools and lodges," as Mary Lynn of the *Cleveland Call and Post* reported after seeing the exhibit at the Western Reserve Historical Society. Blacks were scientists, writers, poets, artists, captains, physicians, and rebels, Lynn noted, thinking the traveling show "made known the awareness and pride that has been a part of the Black culture for centuries."[233]

It might not have had the cachet of the Smithsonian, but the Harlem Institute of Fashion was also demonstrating African

A model wearing a dress designed by activist (and seamstress) Rosa Parks at a Bicentennial fashion show in New York City, October 1975.

Americans' contributions to the national memory. Fashions by Lois Bell (one of New York City's most acclaimed designers), Mary Lou Chandler (who dressed some of the city's richest and most famous ladies), and Ann Lowe (best known for designing the wedding party of Jacqueline Bouvier and John F. Kennedy) were included in the show put together for the Bicentennial.[234]

The Bicentennial Is Everywhere!

As the controversy over minority participation in the Bicentennial lingered, it became apparent that the event had taken on a new life beginning in July 1975. Being just one year away from July 4, 1976, made the Bicentennial seem that much realer, and all kinds of activities, ranging from fun to serious, increased in volume. "The Bicentennial is everywhere!" proclaimed *Seventeen* magazine that month, providing its readers with a long list of festivals across the United States that were somehow connected to the event.[235] National Public Radio had been in existence just five years, but its more than 150 member stations were busy developing Bicentennial programming. Hour-long documentaries on the network's *The States of the Union* series may not have been as jolly as the Banana Festival in Fulton, Kentucky, or the Crawfish Festival in St. Martinville, Louisiana, but they were certainly informative.[236]

Television producers were now going full speed ahead on the event. NBC announced it would broadcast more than 170 hours of Bicentennial-themed programming between July 1975 and July 1976, sprinkling the event throughout its lineup. The network's *Today* show would cover happenings in each of the fifty states over the next year, and three *Hallmark Hall of Fame* specials were in the works (featuring George Washington, Abraham Lincoln, and Harry Truman). There would be much more, as the Bicentennial was weaved into many other shows, including NBC's broadcast of the Miss America Pageant and the Macy's Thanksgiving Day Parade.[237]

In these pre-cable days, network television broadcasts consistently reached millions or even tens of millions of viewers, further integrating the Bicentennial into everyday life in America. Red, white, and blue were of course the dominant colors associated with the event, and they were liberally used on virtually any object. Clothing, especially uniforms, were being increasingly produced in the flag's three colors because of demand from communities, companies, and schools, making them a ubiquitous sight across

Fannie Lee Teals of Tifton, Georgia, with her red, white, and blue American Revolution Bicentennial quilt in 1977.

Members of Girl Scout Troop #2019 of Portland, Connecticut, presenting a Bicentennial Quilt they made to White House Coordinator of Bicentennial Affairs Milt Mitler on the North Lawn of the White House on July 1, 1976.

the country. Tellers in a credit union in Cedar Rapids, Iowa, were wearing red, white, and blue unforms, for example, as were security guards at La Guardia Airport. Marching bands were not only going tricolor but also wearing three-cornered hats and coats with tails, as Minutemen had done. Manufacturers were of course pleased to see what they called "the biggest mobilization of uniforms since World War II," as it was helping revive the American clothing industry which had been hit hard by the recession.[238]

Some were making red, white, and blue uniforms and other clothing by sewing the articles themselves, analogous to the huge crafting industry dedicated to the Bicentennial. Quilting was an especially popular craft, with all kinds of American-centric designs incorporated into the multilayered textiles. There was only one official Bicentennial quilt, however, meaning it was authorized by the ARBA. The "Bicentennial Star Quilt," as it was called, could be had in kit form from *Good Housekeeping* magazine. The design was a combination of traditional quilting and patchwork motifs along with the ARBA's new insignia—a white star surrounding its pretzel-inspired, corporate-like symbol. The quilt, which could be sewed by hand or machine-stitched, came in various sizes, and matching pillow and pillow shams were available.[239]

Professional football players had not all swapped their usual uniforms for red, white, and blue costumes, but they had added Bicentennial emblems to the shoulders of their jerseys. In August 1975, the National Football League became the first professional sports organization to receive official recognition from the ARBA, with its sponsorship to come in various ways. In addition to the patches, both the Hall of Fame game in Canton, Ohio, and Super Bowl X in Miami were certified as official Bicentennial events. There was even an NFL/Bicentennial Scholarship essay contest for high schoolers, the topic being "The NFL's Role in American History." Top prize for the winning five- to seven-hundred-word essay was a $10,000 college scholarship (and a trip to the Super Bowl).[240]

The ARBA/NFL partnership was a natural fit, but not everyone was finding it easy to trade on the publicity being generated by the Bicentennial. The nation's scientific community was feeling especially left out, as there had been precious little attention given to the major contribution of science and technology to the nation's history. "It is ironic that most Americans will see out 1976 knowing little more about American science than the usual lore about Benjamin Franklin and Thomas Jefferson," Constance Holden lamented in *Science*, concluding that "the official Bicentennial structure is not designed to encourage any coherent assessment of the role of science and technology in the United States." There had been talk of creating and setting off a firecracker powerful enough to be seen from the moon, but this was hardly the stuff of serious science. "Historical and artistic endeavors have been moving apace but science had missed the boat," Holden sighed.[241]

Holden had a good point. People from a variety of backgrounds were invited to weigh in on the significance of the Bicentennial from a historical standpoint, usually showing how the event was as much about the nation's future as its past. Plenty could be learned from a closer familiarity with the circumstances of the American Revolution, some of those with an appreciation for the past advised, with all Americans to gain valuable lessons in the principles of democracy. "What better way to celebrate our two hundredth anniversary than by using part of the time, energy, and money expended for the observance to make a serious study of how the American experience in the era of the Revolution might be applied to the future of mankind?" asked Bruno Bitker, a notable Wisconsin attorney and member of that state's Bicentennial Observance Commission.[242]

The flood of Bicentennial souvenirs inundating the American marketplace definitely leaned more toward frivolity than a serious study of the relevance of the Revolution. The ARBA had been largely successful in controlling which American companies were officially licensed to use its symbol (seventy-seven companies were so authorized in September 1975) but there was no way it could stop foreign companies from jumping on the opportunity. Firms in Taiwan and Japan were the most to blame for the plastic Liberty Bells and faux whiskey bottles that included the ARBA symbol, and there didn't seem to a solution to the problem. The ARBA had so far issued cease-and-desist orders against twenty-four companies that had been using the symbol without permission, and all of those firms had complied. Beyond the lack of quality and safety control from foreign makers, the ARBA was missing out on the fees it charged American manufacturers (four to 15 percent of sales) to employ its symbol.[243]

Although it was less enforced, the ARBA was also assigned the responsibility to designate any and all Bicentennial programs being pursued by communities, organizations, or individuals as official. As of July 24, 1975, there were 5,368 ARBA-approved programs, a number that all seemed happy with. Of course, the programs ranged widely in scope and expenditures; Denver was spending $87 million on city improvements, while a small town in Montana had committed to getting a dial phone system by July 4, 1976.[244]

The thousands of programs taking place or in the planning stages helped make Americans want to have something to remember the Bicentennial by. By September 1975, sales of Bicentennial items were high, this despite an economy that had yet to fully recover from the recession. "Cash-register sales are proving that—economic hard times or not—thousands of Americans are celebrating the nation's 200th birthday by snapping up products with almost any bicentennial connection," noted Lucia Mouat of the *Christian Science Monitor*. Critics of commercialism could understand the desire for a medal, commemorative spoon, or a reproduction of an issue of the *Pennsylvania Gazette* to, as the latter was advertised, "read exactly what the colonists read." But was there any need for things like Bicentennial lawn chairs, neckties, and playing cards?[245]

In our consumer society, the marketing possibilities were nearly endless. Banks were offering "Bicentennial savings plans" while airlines were pitching "Bicentennial Air Fares." The maker of a nondairy creamer was saying in its ads, "Coffee Rich started a revolution in good taste," while d-CON, a manufacturer of insecticides, was claiming to be "the people who are helping to free America from bugs."[246] Some in Congress weren't pleased to see what could be interpreted as a sacred event turned into promotional fodder, but others saw it simply as American free enterprise at work. Certain Americans who had been out of the country for a year or two were shocked to see the degree to which Bicentennial-mania had taken over the retail arena. Representations of Revolutionary War heroes were being used to sell toothpaste and lightbulbs, something that more patriotic citizens found discomforting.[247]

We, the People

Where was the line, if there was one, in terms of commercializing or popularizing the Bicentennial? It wasn't clear, but Americans were determined to overlay their particular passion with flag-inspired colors, a wistful throwback to more innocent times. In the fall of 1975, for instance, gardening enthusiasts were planting specially bred bulbs that would the following spring bloom into red, white, and blue Stars and Stripes Hyacinths, red-on-white Union Jack Tulips, and yellow Liberty Bell Daffodils. Bulb and seed companies as well as local gardening centers and nurseries were finding there to be strong consumer interest in such Bicentennialesque flora.[248]

Like collecting colonial-era antiques and making crafts reminiscent of that period, pre–twentieth century American folk art was experiencing a boom because of the Bicentennial. Prices for folk art had gone up dramatically due to increased demand, inflation, and greater interest from an international market that viewed it as distinctly American. While new works were being discovered in attics and barns, the supply was naturally limited, this too raising the value of eighteenth- and nineteenth-century quilts and stoneware. As on the future television show *Antiques Roadshow*, owners of a New England pie plate might discover that that piece of pottery they've been using to hold their car keys was worth more than $1,000, quite a revelation.[249]

For those families who wanted to celebrate the Bicentennial more directly than by growing red, white, and blue flowers or collecting old weathervanes, the big question they were likely to ask was "Should we go somewhere?" If the answer to that question was yes, the obvious follow-up was "Where to?" Some had made definite plans of one kind or another, but many others remained on the fence, not at all sure where to point their car. The lack of a single defining event such as the proposed world's fairs made the decision a difficult one, especially since there was likely to be some sort of celebration right in one's hometown. A good number of Americans were understandably nervous about traveling during the spring or summer of 1976, having seen or heard the predictions of millions of tourists descending on certain historic sites. The government, travel industry, and ARBA all acknowledged these concerns and were providing assistance in various ways.[250]

Tossing the kids in the station wagon and heading to the nation's capital was a common and reasonable choice. There was always a lot to see in Washington, and the city was making a special effort to attract tourists after its series of failed, overambitious efforts. Better to go in 1975 than 1976, however, assuming the findings from a new survey were even close to being accurate. Some twenty-seven million Americans intended to visit the nation's capital in 1976, according to the survey conducted by the U.S. Travel Data Center commissioned by the ARBA, much more than the total of seventeen million estimated by government officials. Lodging would be a problem based on the twenty-seven million figure, but the survey suggested that other key destinations—notably Philadelphia, Boston, New York, and Williamsburg, Virginia—would also experience more tourism than anticipated.[251]

If making the trip to Washington in 1975 or 1976, a must stop was the Smithsonian's National Museum of History and Technology to take in *We, the People*, a show curated especially for the Bicentennial. (The museum became the National Museum of American History in 1980.) The Smithsonian had been nicknamed "the nation's attic" due to its unsurpassed collection of Americana, so curators had much to draw from. The artifacts selected fell into three categories that borrowed a phrase from Lincoln's Gettysburg Address: those "of," "by," and "for" the people. Visitors could see everything from a mother-of-pearl depiction of Mount Vernon to the bathrobe and hairbrush used by John F. Kennedy while he campaigned for president.[252]

A good number of Americans were curating their own historical collections by creating a time capsule. The idea was to fill a container with contemporary artifacts that would be opened (presumably by someone else) on July 4, 2076—the nation's Tricentennial. Individuals, families, and whole communities (even tiny ones such as Plentywood, Montana, and Bell Terre, New York) were pursuing the projects, which might go into an attic or be buried in the ground. Coins, newspaper clippings, and campaign buttons were typical items included, although some were taking a more innovative approach. Delta, Colorado, collected local citizens' signatures (at a penny apiece) and put those along with a savings bank passbook with a value of $100

TOP: *We the People*, which opened at the National Museum of American History on June 4, 1975, celebrated Americans' freedom of speech, including voices of protest against war and discrimination based on race and gender. BOTTOM: Treasures from the past were displayed in glass cases like these.

in its capsule—a fiberglass coffin that was buried in the town's cemetery. With a century of compound interest, the $100 would be worth $15,000 in 2076, a banker estimated.[253]

Paying a penny to be put on Delta, Colorado's registry for posterity was a legitimate endeavor, but there were plenty of Bicentennial scams taking place. Someone was selling inclusion in a "Bicentennial registry" in the National Archives for $1, which came as news to people at the government agency, since they had no such plan. One phony travel company was taking reservations for a "Bicentennial cruise" aboard the *SS United States*, the problem being that the ship had been mothballed in 1969. A "Miss Bicentennial" beauty contest was also being promoted, with hopefuls later disappointed to learn their $15 entry fee went to naught. There were so many of these kinds of cons taking place that the Better Business Bureau took time to warn consumers about anything being sold that had "Bicentennial" in its name.[254]

Editors of *Better Homes and Gardens* may have been tempted to call their new publication the *Bicentennial Cook Book*, but they wisely went with the *Heritage Cook Book* as a "salute to the nation's first 200 years." (The Junior League of Philadelphia did indeed publish a *Bicentennial Cookbook* with recipes contributed by members.) Released just in time for Thanksgiving 1975, the book offered seven hundred recipes that drew from different historical periods over the course of four hundred years. The cookbook would come in especially handy for Americans wishing to celebrate the Bicentennial by including in their Thanksgiving meal foods that the Indians, Pilgrims, the Pennsylvania Dutch, and the Shakers might have eaten.[255]

For *Woman's Day*, meanwhile, superstar chef James Beard offered his own take on making a "Tribute-to-America Thanksgiving," with wild turkey the centerpiece of the feast.[256] A month later, with the year-end holidays approaching, *Ladies' Home Journal* offered a guide to "Spirits of '76," i.e., "the cups of cheer our forefathers concocted in order to brace the backbone of democracy." Readers learned how to make drinks such as hot buttered cider and John Adams' New England Eggnog, the latter being, according to the magazine, "a Colonial favorite that will be a hit at any Yuletide gathering."[257]

Redbook, another leading women's magazine, was taking a different tack that November, however. Serving one's family nutmeg squash, candied cranberries, and Ohio lemon pie was certainly a nice way to celebrate the Bicentennial, but for Bess Myerson, there were, well, bigger fish to fry. Myerson, whose résumé included having been the first Miss America, many television appearances, and an impressive political career, reminded readers that women had played a major role in the founding of America. Not just the Founding Fathers but Abigail Adams, Martha Jefferson, and many other women helped shape the contours of the new nation, although there was still much to do two hundred years later. "As we approach our Bicentennial there is a lengthy agenda of unfinished business for the democracy we celebrate," she wrote, urging women to join the struggle for "equal rights and full participation in every facet of American life."[258]

From Minutemen to Spacemen

"Equal Rights for Women" would likely be Myerson's submission to what was turning out to be an incredibly popular Bicentennial slogan contest. The contest, called "Slogans USA," was sponsored by columnist Jack Anderson, who had in September 1974 asked his readers to "Put into words our feelings about America to shake off the dirt of Watergate and think constructively about our country." Ten thousand submissions a week arrived in Anderson's office in Washington, DC, so much mail that the columnist had dozens of volunteers from the Jaycees, the American Legion, and the Federation of Women's Clubs screen them. The one hundred best entries would be sent to the heads of the fifty-five state and territorial commissions, who would choose the six finalists. Those half-dozen people and their entries would be announced at the January 18, 1976 Super Bowl; in Anderson's column; and in *Time*, *Newsweek*, *TV Guide*, and other magazines. After that the contest was determined by popular vote, with the winner to receive a brand new 1976 station wagon, a thirty-day tour of the United States courtesy of Holiday Inn, and $5,000 in spending money.[259]

There were more than one million submissions by the time the contest closed in December 1975, making choosing a winner a difficult process, to say the very least. Some of the more interesting entries were: "From Minutemen to Spacemen"; "America Is Like Frosted Flakes, It's Great"; and "I Get High on Apple Pie." All fifty states were represented, with some entries written in needlepoint. Children were heavily represented in the contest, which served as a popular elementary school classroom activity.[260]

Although it was definitely the biggest, "Slogans USA" was one of many contests or competitions staged for the nation's Bicentennial. In December 1975 in Chicago, for example, there was what was billed as a "challenging Bicentennial happening" aired on local television station WBBM. Covering two hundred years of American history, *The Great American History Test* pitted fifty contestants against each other to see who could answer the most multiple choice or true or false questions correctly. News anchorman Bill Kurtis served as cohost, and various famous figures such as Senator Adlai Stevenson, actress Ginger Rogers, and baseball star Willie Mays posed questions via videotape.[261]

Most of the contestants on *The Great American History Test* were local college students, a reflection of the effort made to make the Bicentennial meaningful for young people. States such as Michigan held essay contests for high school seniors on the relevance of the Bicentennial to current events, with cash going toward a college scholarship the top prize. In the case of Michigan, a bonus was added for the winning essay: a self-composed "Bicentennial Minute" that would be nationally broadcast on CBS as part of its continuing series. (A trip to Williamsburg, Virginia, was also thrown in.) Linda Gayle Rodgers, who happened to be Black, was one of two finalists in Michigan's contest, and her essay focused on whether African Americans should participate in the Bicentennial. "Neither a pessimistic philosophy nor a false optimism will further the American dream of freedom and justice for all," Rodgers wrote, arguing that "a constructive, realistic effort to build upon the foundation provided 200 years ago must be promulgated."[262]

Rodgers' words were wise, but not everyone could relate to them. "How can we genuinely observe a 200th birthday anniversary as a democratic nation?" asked Bernice Shelton, a *Baltimore Afro-American* correspondent, finding no justification for African Americans like herself to celebrate the Bicentennial.[263] Efforts were still being made to demonstrate Blacks' contributions to the progress of the nation, however. The Association for the Study of Afro-American Life and History, for example, had announced a program in which bronze markers would be placed at more than one hundred sites across the country where a notable event led by Blacks took place.[264]

Many other such projects were in progress, the ARBA was proud to say in its newsletter the *Bicentennial Times*. An NAACP-sponsored Pennsylvania Bicentennial Human Relations Congress would be held in 1976, and the largest collection of Black history materials in Florida was being built in Jacksonville. Delaware State College was holding African American heritage–related lectures, performing arts shows, and "ethnic days," and a film about Benjamin Banneker, whose accomplishments included being one of the surveyors for the design of Washington, DC, was being made in his hometown of Baltimore. Other projects included a public television special on Black history in Oregon; a series of seminars on notable African American Kansans at the University of Kansas; and a jazz, blues, ragtime, and gospel festival in St. Louis.[265]

Some African Americans were using their personal talents to further bring Black history into the Bicentennial. Miles G. Savage, a twenty-three-year-old television producer in Detroit, for example, was creating a series of one-minute public service announcements featuring interesting facts about the role that Black people had played in that city.[266] Also in Detroit, Flori Roberts, a leading manufacturer of beauty products for African American women, constructed a calendar-booklet of notable Black women in American history. Roberts featured lesser-known women such as concert singer Sissiretta Jones (who had performed in the White House), bank president and newspaperwoman Maggie L. Walker, musical comedy star Florence Mills (credited with introducing the cake-walk dance), sculptress Augusta Savage, artist Laura Wheeling Waring, and organizer Mary Church Terrell.[267]

Gatherings such as Esto '76 (a dance festival in Baltimore organized by the Estonian community) were ways in which Americans demonstrated both ethnic and national pride during the Bicentennial.

Shirley Graham DuBois, wife of the late African American scholar and historian W.E.B. DuBois, agreed that Blacks had a stake in the nation's Bicentennial that shouldn't be overlooked. "It is up to us to refute the lie that the only American history or the only American experience is white," she said in her November 1975 speech at the Jean Baptiste Pointe DuSable Museum (later the DuSable Black History Museum and Education Center) in Chicago.[268] In his own speech made that same month, State Representative David Scott (D-GA) made the compelling case that the fundamental story of the Bicentennial was the struggle for freedom, a story to which African Americans could definitely relate.[269]

Vernon E. Jordan, who had expressed his views on African Americans' recognition of the Bicentennial in *Ebony* and elsewhere, did so again at a conference in St. Louis. "We cannot celebrate," the executive director of the National Urban League said in his talk to the group, "we can only affirm the principles, so often broken and violated, that make up the ideals behind the Declaration of Independence, the Constitution, and the founding of our nation." This was now a running theme of African Americans' attitudes toward the Bicentennial; the doctrines of the American Revolution were truly extraordinary, but that didn't mean that Blacks should take delight in attending the nation's birthday party given their own history.[270]

Writing for *New York Amsterdam News* in December 1975, Father Lawrence E. Lucas nicely summarized three alternative approaches that African Americans were taking toward the Bicentennial. The first was to simply ignore it "on the basis that it's all white folks fun and games"; the second was to go all in on it, as Blacks were as American as anyone; and the third was to celebrate it but with reservations due to racism, past and present, and possibly make a point of demonstrating African Americans' contributions to the nation. Like most others, the Harlem-based Catholic priest and civil rights activist fell into the third camp, seeing that as the most challenging option but the one that aligned most closely with Black Americans' dual identities.[271]

Benjamin E. Mays, however, saw things quite differently. For the ex-president of Morehouse College and advisor to LBJ, African Americans should turn the Bicentennial into something else than a giant pat on the nation's back, meaning it wasn't just a matter of opting out, joining in, or something in between. Using history as a judge, White Americans were simply not capable of creating a moral and ethical society, he proposed, making it Blacks' responsibility to take a leadership role in this all-important pursuit. There was no better time than the Bicentennial for African Americans to begin turning the country into a virtuous place, Mays argued, hoping that others would embrace this rather unorthodox view.[272] The course of the American Bicentennial was hardly over, however, as the peak of the event neared.

The bicentennial is the most massive volunteer network since World War II.

—John Warner, 1976

4.

Hometown, U.S.A.

In January 1975, Marvin J. Rosenblum was sitting with his wife when he suddenly leaped to his feet and shouted, "Eureka!" What had made the thirty-two-year-old Chicago attorney react so alarmingly? Rosenblum had unexpectedly come up with what he later called the "ultimate Bicentennial idea." The man envisioned a human chain of three to five million people holding hands from Boston to Los Angeles on July 4, 1776, the two hundredth anniversary of the signing of the Declaration of Independence.[273]

It took a full year, but in January 1976 Rosenblum got the chance to meet with John Warner, head of the ARBA, to ask for government help ($2 million) to make his dream come true. Rosenblum had done his homework; roughly 1,320 people per mile would be needed to make the coast-to-coast chain, he told Warner, as a person with outstretched arms averaged four feet in length. Rosenblum was actually not the first person to come up with a transcontinental linking of people for the Bicentennial, as an Illinois woman had suggested the idea to her congressman in 1974. The lawyer copyrighted the concept and created a nonprofit corporation around it, however, giving him ownership of what he called "a Mount Rushmore of emotion" and "a national Woodstock." Rosenblum also saw his "Great Wall of American People" as analogous to the Great Wall of China.[274]

Would a national "Hands Across America" turn out to be the defining event for the Bicentennial that many thought was needed as a unifying theme? Warner liked the idea and pledged support by the ARBA but made no commitments.[275]

Voices of America

With a new session of Congress opening in January 1976, politicos could not help but locate the Bicentennial within the context of big government. The number of federal civilian employees had mushroomed to almost three million, and more than two hundred new federal departments, agencies, and bureaus had sprung up since 1960. Most concerning was the cost of running the government, which had almost quadrupled since John F. Kennedy's inauguration. Was this what the Founding Fathers had in mind when forming a government focused on the people as opposed to the way that the British monarchy operated?[276]

A revolt against the government was highly unlikely, but along with national pride, there was a fair amount of uneasiness and dismay among the American people. That's what Roderick Nordell of the *Christian Science Monitor* reported after he traveled coast to coast to get the pulse of the nation as the Bicentennial continued to gain traction. For his "Voices of America" piece, Nordell interviewed hundreds of folks to get a sense of "the spirit of 1976."

Those who saw the glass half empty pointed to rising crime and government corruption while those who saw the glass half full suggested that the United States would be very much around in another two hundred years.

One particular voice of America saw our glass as nearly overflowing. "We are the richest nation in the world—rich in our resources, rich in our creativity, rich in our strength, and rich in our people," President Ford said in his official proclamation that 1976 was the "Bicentennial Year." There were challenges ahead, of course, but inspiration could be found though the actions of our forebears who had founded the country. "As we enter America's third century," Ford stated, "let us emulate in word and deed, their resolve and vision."[278]

After a decade of planning, it was good to have the federal government's official endorsement of the American Bicentennial. Regardless, however, individuals and organizations were moving ahead with their own ways to celebrate the event. No details had been released, but an insider source (going by the name of "Raw Throat") leaked that the Rolling Stones were planning a summer Bicentennial tour of the United States.[279] The Bicentennial had also worked itself into *Sesame Street*, the still experimental education series for preschoolers airing on public television stations. (The show had begun in 1969.) In one episode, Big Bird runs for president, in the process learning the ways of the American political system, and in another Count von Count comes to know the role of business in society through, naturally, counting. More episodes were planned, each one based on a topic being addressed in the American Issues Forum.[280]

NBC, meanwhile, was airing something completely different: *Under God*, which consisted of eight hour-long specials that were related to the Bicentennial and presented by four religious organizations (the National Council of Churches, the Southern Baptist Convention, the Jewish Theological Seminary of America, and the United States Catholic Conference). Religious life was central to the history of the United States and to the world, the series showed, something important to remember during the Bicentennial year.[281]

A worthy pursuit, no doubt, but it was clear that the Bicentennial was being used as a vehicle for many interest groups to promote themselves. Organizations with no real connection to the Bicentennial were staging some kind of event or contest that was likely to get attention to in order to get free publicity. The junior division of the National Humane Society, for example, sponsored an election to name America's favorite "bicentennial animal," a dubious effort. Surprisingly, the bald eagle did not finish first in the voting. (The bird had, after all, been chosen as the national symbol by the Second Continental Congress in 1782.) It was the horse that received the most votes from children across the country as the "bicentennial animal," followed by the bald eagle, white-tailed deer, buffalo, grizzly bear, whale, wolf, cattle, coyote, beaver, mule, and salmon.[282]

There were many more examples of such silliness, something that Will Lissner felt compelled to comment on in the *American Journal of Economics and Sociology*, of which he served as editor in chief. "Save the U.S. Bicentennial," he urged his readers, thinking that the country's "glorious tradition as a liberty-loving democracy" was being overshadowed by a steady stream of peripheral activities, including faux militarism. Lissner agreed with Edward L. Bernays, the legendary public relations consultant, who had in June 1975 sent a letter to the Boston *Sunday Herald Advertiser* expressing his views on the matter. Bernays was also disturbed by the "marching, musketry and mock mayhem" taking place, thinking that the "sham battles" were doing a disservice to the ideals associated with the American Revolution.[283]

For Clayton Jones of the *Christian Science Monitor*, it was what he called "star-spangled knickknacks" that was ruining the Bicentennial. Even John Warner was worried about the number of knickknacks being sold and that he was powerless to stop it. "Commercialism could be the Achilles heel that brings down the bicentennial," he said, the worse news being that almost all of it was tacky. (A red, white, and blue teddy bear that recited the Declaration of Independence was sadly proving to be quite popular.) By February 1976, the ARBA had licensed 102 manufacturers to use its symbol, but all of those products were "tasteful," according to Warner. (The products included an eighty-five-dollar Paul Revere lantern and a less pricey three-corner hat.) Craftsmen were making their own unique memorabilia, such as a Bicentennial edition Winchester rifle, but those too were wholly acceptable, Warner made clear.[284]

It was perfectly legal for marketers to trade on the Bicentennial as long as they didn't use the ARBA symbol, however, and they were taking full advantage of the opportunity. A short list of new products introduced included: "Uncle Samwiches"; "Spirit of '76" burial caskets; red, white, and blue striped toilet seats; Patriotic Pink lipstick; and Revolutionary cherry pie filling. This was American free enterprise, and the ARBA had no authority to stop it even if they had the resources to. If there was any consolation, it was knowing that the 1876 Centennial had also been heavily commercialized and that the glassware, china, mugs, and trinkets produced for the occasion were now quite valuable as collectors' items.[285] Would a Patriotic Pink lipstick be much sought after in 2076?

Another source of comfort was that despite the exploitation of the Bicentennial, the ARBA was receiving almost $1 million in royalties from its licensed products, adding to the $9.5 million that Congress had appropriated. Some 35,000 programs and events in about 8,500 communities were being funded with that money, a campaign that Warner claimed to be reaching at least 90 percent of Americans. Thirty to forty corporations were paying for larger national programs, but for Warner it was the grassroots projects that made the effort truly remarkable. "This bicentennial will be in Hometown, U.S.A.," he stated, confirming there would be no single spectacle as some still wanted. The Boy Scouts and a number of radio deejays were backing the "Hands Across America" idea, but the ARBA was not actively pursuing it.[286]

Instead of holding some all-encompassing event, Warner recommended that Americans celebrate the Bicentennial over a period of four days over a long Fourth of July weekend. (July 4 fell on a Sunday in 1976.) Day 1 should focus on the Revolution, making it fitting for families to read the Declaration of Independence together; Day 2 could be an occasion to consider the country's religious heritage; Day 3 would feature the big party, filled with fireworks (John Adams himself called for pyrotechnics to mark the event); and Day 4 would serve as an appropriate time to think about America's future and how to make it a good one.[287]

Just as Warner had said, however, millions of Americans were already embarking on their programs in their own ways. In Newington, Connecticut, for example, students at Elm Hill and Center Schools had designated February 1976 as their month to observe the Bicentennial. Fifth graders at the former school designed their own Bicentennial flags in art class, and each week a different theme in American history was expressed through music and food. (One week was the "Cowboy Era.") At Center School, meanwhile, a colonial tavern that served apple cider was created; the students themselves had made the cider the previous fall.[288]

The Real Spirit of America

Lin Hilburn, a journalist for the *Los Angeles Sentinel*, would likely have agreed that the activities being pursued in Newington, Connecticut, reflected what he called "the real spirit of America." Hilburn, an African American, had his own identifiers of the country's real spirit against the backdrop of the Bicentennial, citing equal opportunity, parents making sacrifices for the benefit of their children, and the brave acts of Harriet Tubman, Martin Luther King Jr., and Medgar Evers. "It is the spirit of Americans of all colors, of all religions, of all backgrounds that says a man's worth cannot be measured by the color of his skin," Hilburn poetically wrote, thinking that 1976 was an ideal time to embrace that perspective.[289]

Equal opportunity did not seem to apply in the many Bicentennial television specials being broadcast, however. For Jews, there was *Where We Came From* and Native Americans had *I Will Fight No More, Forever*, and every week there seemed to be a show about White colonists leading the American Revolution. "Where are the specials showing what blacks have contributed to the American Revolution and to the building of this nation over the past 200 years?" asked Vashti McKenzie of the *Baltimore Afro-American*. White Americans were ashamed of their treatment of African Americans, McKenzie thought, and shows telling the story would only remind them of their persecution. Black men did indeed fight at Bunker Hill and Lexington and Concord, she reminded her readers, urging them to pressure network executives into making Bicentennial specials about the history of African Americans. Blacks spent a lot of money as consumers, McKenzie correctly pointed out, something of which advertisers might have to be reminded.[290]

To McKenzie's point, there was of course much material from which television producers could draw to present a fairer representation of the American Revolution in terms of race. A case could be made, in fact, that it was Black colonists who more vigorously led the pursuit of "liberty and justice for all," as it was obviously in their interests to do so. The Founding Fathers, on the other hand, signed the Declaration of Independence out of a desire to, according to Joseph Carpenter, "serve the interest of the power elite of Virginia and other colonial industrialists." Writing in the *Negro History Bulletin*, Carpenter concluded that "there is a need for a radical reconstruction of the life and soul of the American Revolution for the Bicentennial of American Independence." [291]

Given the distortion of American history grossly magnified by the media—the Wild West was hardly exclusively White, as shows like *Bonanza* and *Gunsmoke* suggested—did African Africans have a moral obligation to demonstrate their patriotism during the Bicentennial? Ethically bound or not, Blacks had a deep reservoir of history to be proud of, Elmer Eugene Wells made clear in the same issue of the *Negro History Bulletin*. Besides being very much active in the American West of the nineteenth century, Blacks had won the first Kentucky Derby (there were actually fourteen African American riders that day), first planted the American flag on the North Pole, and achieved many other "firsts" that were largely unknown or forgotten. For those African Americans asking the question, "What do we have to celebrate during the Bicentennial?" Wells replied, "We have as much to celebrate as anybody—perhaps a little more."[292]

The Association for the Study of Afro-American Life and History (ASALH) apparently thought similarly. "Black History Week" had been established in 1926 by Carter G. Woodson, founder of that organization, but in the Bicentennial year the ASALH declared February "Black History Month." Schools and colleges would recognize Black heritage, achievements, and future goals through the month of February, the ASALH announced, the beginnings of Black History Month observations that continue to this day.[293]

Black history would be a major part of the 1976 edition of ON TOUR, a traveling Bicentennial program organized by the Smithsonian Institution. ON TOUR brought elements of the cultural heritage of some forty countries to cities and towns across the United States to "create a local celebration that reflects the unique ethnic experience within each community." Having been successful in the summer of 1975, ON TOUR was being expanded for the summer of 1976. Smithsonian field researchers and foreign folklorists selected dancers, singers, musicians, and craftspeople considered to be representative of the folk traditions of each nation, and then community groups, arts councils, parks, museums, and universities could engage the performers. There would be two ON TOUR programs in 1976: *Old Ways in the New World*, which focused on Americans of European Asian, and Hispanic descent, and *African Diaspora*, which examined "the continuity of the Black experience from Africa to the United States, the Caribbean, and Latin America."[294]

Two Knox College students in Galesburg, Illinois, were taking an alternative approach to, in their own words, "get closer to the meaning of the bicentennial." Dan Keith, a senior, and Brian Fischer, a junior, were spending two months in an Indian-style teepee to gain a better understanding of Native American life of two centuries ago. The pair slept and cooked in the eight-foot teepee, which was on the college campus, but used their fraternity's washroom for hygiene purposes and the library for studying. "We've seen a lot of the commercial ideas about the bicentennial," Fischer told a reporter, thinking "they really didn't get down to the basic point."[295]

A Bicentennial project of a much different sort was taking shape in Pulaski, Tennessee. The Ku Klux Klan was planning a national rally in that town, where the group had first been formed in 1865 (in a law office, of all places). "We're going to have wagon trains from just about every state," boasted Dan Henson, grand dragon of the Tennessee Chapter of the United Klans of America, apparently taking inspiration from the "Bicentennial Wagon Train Pilgrimage" destined for Valley Forge. The May 1976 Klan rally would last just one day, Henson added, but the group optimistically predicted that fifty thousand members would attend.[296]

Happily, local Bicentennial commissions were funding projects that celebrated the diversity of America. In March 1976, for example, the District of Columbia Office of Bicentennial Programs awarded grants to twenty-one neighborhood projects, with money that had come from the ARBA specifically for that purpose. The projects included outdoor murals reflecting Chinese American, African American, and Latin American heritages, and there were programs for older adults, people with disabilities, and the deaf as well. Yet another project located at Frederick Douglass's former home had muralists reproduce the geometric ones in Zulu villages in Africa.[297]

Greater attention to the diversity of America could be detected through Bicentennial activities as July 4 drew closer and closer. Projects and programs were widely scattered, but it appeared that multiculturalism was emerging as a central theme of the event. "Americans are a blend of divergent nationalities—and so is our cooking," began a March 1976 article in *Better Homes and Gardens*, a good example of the shift in approach. Editors of the magazine had decided to "dip into the ethnic melting pot for our Bicentennial tribute to American cooking," first by sharing the holiday food customs of four families of European ancestry (German, Norwegian, Greek, and Dutch). A follow-up article featured the cuisine of Native American, Indian American, Chinese American, and Jewish American families that had been handed down over the generations.[298]

The swing toward diversity could also be seen in *Heritage Days: The Black Perspective*, which would open in June at Harpers Ferry National Park in West Virginia. The "tribute to the contributions of Black Americans," as it was described by the *Atlanta Daily World*, was sponsored by the ASALH along with the Storer College Alumni Association. (Between 1867 and 1955, Storer College had been a major institution of higher education for Blacks in the United States.) The three-day program, which was open to the public, included exhibits, dramatic and musical presentations, and seminars by an all-star cast of African American speakers including Georgia State Senator Julian Bond; Congresswoman Shirley Chisholm of New York; Congressman Andrew Young of Georgia; Benjamin Quarles, professor of history at Morgan State University; and Roy Wilkins, executive director of the NAACP.[299]

Where Is the Bicentennial?

Better late than never, one might say with regard to the higher profile of American diversity in the run-up to July 4. Still, it was the thirty thousand or so projects across the United States that were defining the American Bicentennial, something Margot Hornblower of the *Washington Post* called "home-grown celebrations." "Everybody asks me, 'Where is the Bicentennial?'" John Warner commented—his response, "It's in your community!" Geographically spreading out the Bicentennial was taking some of the pressure off Boston, Washington, and Philadelphia, whose city officials had fretted about overcrowding.[300]

The worries among New Englanders that the area would be swamped with tourists appeared so far to be unwarranted. Hotel bookings were up over 1975 but not nearly what the Chicken Littles had predicted, in part because Boston tourism officials had decided not to heavily promote the Bicentennial due to budget trimmings and a feeling that "they'll come anyway." States such as Pennsylvania, Virginia, and now New York were spending heavily, stealing some of the thunder of Massachusetts and its neighbors.[301]

In fact, there were signs that New York City, which hadn't even put in a bid for a giant exposition, was going to steal the Bicentennial show. "The biggest bicentennial event of 1976 is coming from abroad—under the taut, billowing sails of more than 225 sailing vessels," exclaimed Jack Miner in the *Christian Science Monitor*. The Operation Sail armada would come into New York Harbor on July 4 and later enter other major ports in the United States. It was said that there hadn't been such a sizable flotilla since the 1600s, and it would be the first time in the twentieth century that the harbor would be closed to commercial traffic. "Tall ships," as the wind-driven square riggers were commonly called, would be arriving from Great Britain, Italy, Denmark, Norway, Poland, the Netherlands, West Germany, Japan, Chile, Spain, and the Soviet Union.[302]

The millions of people expected to come to New York City to see the ships might want to include the Metropolitan Museum of Art on their itinerary. The Met was offering a much-edited version of *A Bicentennial Treasury: American Masterpieces from the Metropolitan*, which was billed as the finest American collection of art on the planet. There would be more than ten thousand fine and decorative art objects in that show, the catch being that the Met's American Bicentennial Wing wouldn't be ready to house the collection until 1978. Until then, the museum's exhibition was just a little more than one hundred objects, but the show's high quality was said to more than make up for its low quantity.[303]

For Philadelphia, New York would be a tough act to follow, even given the former's unparalleled history as the birthplace of the nation. Philadelphia was not only where the Continental Congress met in Independence Hall to adopt the Declaration of Independence in July 1776 but also where the first United States Congress met in 1791 and where the United States Supreme Court sat in the 1790s. (It had of course also been the site of the Centennial Exposition of 1876.) A century later, ceremonies were planned, of course, but for pure wow effect, New York appeared to be unbeatable as a place for tourists to come.[304]

Washington, DC, meanwhile, had seemed to settle primarily on its ace in the hole—the museums and historic buildings on the Mall. The *Nation of Nations* show at the Museum of History and Technology would no doubt draw many visitors, as would the new National Air and Space Museum. A multimedia presentation

A U.S. Army honor guard dressed as Continental soldiers for the opening of an exhibit on the Bicentennial of that branch of the military called *The Creation of an American Army*.

called *The American Adventure* at the National Heritage Theater also appeared to be tourist friendly. Visitors would also be happy to see a new subway system, two new visitors' centers, and a new public garden.[305] Boston was countering with an interactive exhibit called *The Revolution* in the Quincy Market Building, the self-explanatory *Victorian Boston* at the First Corps of Cadets Armory (better known as "The Castle"), and *Where's Boston*, a show about the modern city, at the Prudential Center. There was also of course the Boston Tea Party Ship and Museum and some other mainstays.[306]

Already on the road was the U.S. Armed Forces Bicentennial Caravan, a traveling exhibit presenting *The History of the American Armed Forces and Their Contributions to the Nation*. The caravan consisted of four vans, each one dedicated to one of the branches of the military (Army, Navy, Marine Corps, and Air Force). The exhibit was designed to be educational and entertaining rather than a recruiting effort.[307]

As Americans made their Bicentennial plans, the White House was receiving hundreds of gifts commemorating the event. More than seven hundred such gifts had arrived by April 1976, an eclectic array of objects that the White House had not solicited in any way. Some were professionally crafted while others were, well, less than professionally made (often by schoolchildren). In addition to the gifts, which included a model of the *USS Constitution* ("Old Ironsides"), a set of Revolutionary War soldiers made from clothespins, a ceramic eagle (sent from West Germany), a crocheted flag (one of many), and a *papier-mâché* Betsy Ross, some fifty thousand letters had been sent to President Ford himself, each one in support of the United States.[308]

A commemorative hand-crafted depiction of a Union Eagle mounted on a wooden frame. The eagle is made from wild bird seed and rice and is signed by the artist, Ramona Winchell, and dated 1976.

LEFT: A black leather belt with a brass, commemorative Bicentennial belt buckle with "USA / 200" printed in script along with images of the Liberty Bell and the Spirit of '76. RIGHT: This commemorative silver ring displays a relief figure of an eagle in flight. The sides of the ring read "1776-1976," and the name "Ardavast" is engraved on the inside of the ring.

TOP: This Bicentennial commemorative edition of the Holy Bible titled the "Freedom Edition" consists of the King James Version of the Bible with blue leather binding. The cover is embossed with an antiquated gold-tone Liberty Bell in an oval seal. It was published by the Regency Publishing house in Nashville, Tennessee. BOTTOM: A box of fifteen billiard balls created to commemorate the Bicentennial. This set is series #0001 of a limited edition. The cue ball has the dates "1776 / 1976" printed on its surface; the other balls are numbered 1 through 14.

A commemorative bowl made of over 150 ounces of sterling silver and lined with 24-karat gold. The bowl features a frieze of the nation's two-hundred-year history, from the signing of the Declaration of Independence to the Bicentennial celebration. The bowl is a limited edition and is numbered 1 of 750 made. The donor to the Gerald R. Ford Library was Frank L. Rizzo, the mayor of Philadelphia.

LEFT: A commemorative pin from the representatives of Michigan's bicentennial commission. The pin features a blue stylized "76" with an image of the state of Michigan depicted in silver on a red circular background on top. The pin is mounted in a green felt box with a white silk-lined lid. RIGHT: This silver pocket watch has the Seal of the President depicted on the front set with colored stones. The watch face features a silver background with gold details. The pocket watch sits inside a silver box lined with blue velvet.

TOP LEFT: A commemorative pewter Bicentennial thermometer depicting a hand-engraved eagle above a laurel wreath with the dates "1776" and "1976" written inside. Below are embossed metric and Fahrenheit scales. Included with the thermometer was a copper-colored box with silver-colored writing. TOP RIGHT: A commemorative Bicentennial rawhide necklace decorated with wooden beads and actual shark teeth. The pendant is a decorative arrowhead with a carved American eagle and reads, "200 / 1776-1976." BOTTOM: A pressed wooden plaque commemorating the Bicentennial decorated with a decoupage facsimile of the Declaration of Independence on one side and an "astrological chart of America" on the opposing side. Colored stickers and printed-paper decorate the plaque.

This red, white, and blue cash register was originally used on the Freedom Train. A plaque on the register above the keys reads, "This R.C. Allen Electronic Cash Register was utilized on the American Freedom Train during its epic journey throughout the United States in commemoration of our Nation's Bicentennial / 1776-1976."

A wood bicentennial purse coated with several coats of lacquer. The outside of the purse has images that portray Revolutionary War scenes. The inside of the purse is lined with blue velvet.

A handmade Bicentennial wooden box painted blue and decorated with patriotic images including the Seal of the President and images of George Washington and Thomas Jefferson. Red suede lines the inside and the inside cover is inscribed: "Mayor and Mrs. Lawrence F. Kramer – June 6, 1976." Lawrence R. Kramer, the mayor of Paterson, New Jersey, presented the commemorative box to President Ford during the president's trip to New Jersey.

A handcrafted miniature cannon made out of brass with a wooden frame, ornamented with brass studs. Engraved plaques on either side of the frame translate to, "To Mr. President, Gerald R. Ford. A souvenir on the occasion of the 200th anniversary of the American Revolution / Poland / J. Radwanski / 1976."

TOP LEFT: A ceramic figurine of Betsy Ross sewing the American flag poured by Ed Crowley and hand-painted by his wife for the Bicentennial. The flag is covered with strips of felt. BOTTOM LEFT: Six different Bicentennial buttons designed and sent by two art teachers to President Ford. Each button contains an individual design in red, white, and blue featuring various patriotic images and slogans. RIGHT: Duncan Miller originally manufactured the parking meter, but the Koontz Equipment Corporation turned it into a lamp. The lamp is painted red, white, and blue with flags printed with the dates 1776–1976.

Many Bicentennial events included fireworks, of course, a fitting thing not only for the oohs and aahs but because George Washington happened to love them as well. There were growing concerns about the safety of the things, however, as there would likely be more explosives set off for the Bicentennial than the during the Revolutionary War itself. The Consumer Product Safety Commission was trying to ban any firework with more than fifty milligrams of powder, and the Bureau of Alcohol, Tobacco, and Firearms was cracking down on the bootleg M-80s and skyrockets being produced in remote factories. It had been made illegal to advertise fireworks on children's television, but demand for them still exceeded supply. Devotees of pyrotechnics argued that limiting fireworks displays on, before, or after July 4 was "un-American," but emergency rooms were bracing themselves for what might be a very busy night.[309]

Hospitals in Washington, DC, were hopefully staffing up, as it was soon announced that the biggest fireworks display in American history would take place in that city over the July 4 weekend. The biggest float parade in the nation's history would also be held that weekend, a clear sign that city officials (and a nonprofit group called Happy Birthday USA!) realized they were being outshone by New York and arguably Boston and Philadelphia.[310] That the nation's capital had stepped up its game was a good thing, although it made a difficult decision even more difficult: Where would the president of the United States spend the Bicentennial? Wherever Ford went, John Warner would be with him, the latter made clear, as he wanted to see his boss's reactions firsthand.[311]

If Ford and Warner decided to stay in their hometown from late June through early July, they might run into a group celebrating the Bicentennial in their own fashion. The West Coast–based

Call Off Your Old Tired Ethics (COYOTE) decided to hold its first International Hookers' Convention in Washington, DC, over those weeks, knowing that there would be plenty of business to be had. The group had chosen the nation's capital to meet for another reason. Margo St. James, its leader, was starting a national campaign to decriminalize prostitution, and Washington was the logical place to lobby in support of the cause. In fact, James made the case that prostitution was actually already legal in the United States but in an unofficial sense: "marriage."[312]

A Worldwide Event

As the Bicentennial assumed greater proportions, James M. Banner Jr., an American history professor at Princeton University, felt the need to call a time-out. Why have the Bicentennial? he asked, citing the long list of bobbles that had been made ever since the idea was proposed. Under LBJ's direction, planning for the event had moved at a snail's pace and awkwardly so, and commercialism and partisanship had defined Nixon's managerial style. Now with President Ford and John Warner leading the way, the Bicentennial was basically a ship without a captain, as the ARBA had decided to coordinate state and local efforts rather than launch its own.[313]

Rather than pooh-pooh the idea of a Bicentennial, however, Banner actually posited that it was an important event, at least in theory, as it was a ritual or collective rite like all cultures had. "It is a series of activities, suffused with a sense of the sacred and mysterious past...which call people to a recollection of their past and to their guiding norms," he wrote. There were all sorts of problems with the American Bicentennial that went beyond how it was mismanaged, however, the main one being that the Revolution wasn't easily packaged into a ritualistic form (or as sacred to us as the Civil War). As well, Americans didn't place a high value on history in general, and our heterogeneous society further hurt the chances of creating a Bicentennial that was truly meaningful.[314]

One wonders what Banner would think about some of the Bicentennial activities taking place across the country in the spring of 1976. Hilton Hotels, for example, had begun a daily "Bicentennial flag salute," with all of the hotels in the United States taking part. Each hotel in the chain raised an American flag in the morning and lowered it at night, with all activities paused for one minute so that guests and employees could pay their respect to the occasion. There was also fife and drum music, after which the flag was placed in a special, spotlighted spot until brought out again by a selected employee.[315]

There wasn't much ritual in the "Bikecentennial," which got underway in May 1976, but it was certainly a great way to see the country assuming one had the legs to do it. The transcontinental ride had been carefully planned, as experts in such things had spent three years finding a scenic route that was also relatively easy to pedal. Some six to ten thousand cyclists were expected to embark on the 4,250-mile trip from Yorktown, Virginia, to Astoria, Oregon. More than eighty "Bike Inns" had been set up in school gyms, churches, and college dorms, and hundreds of cafés and restaurants had pledged to feed the hungry cyclists.[316]

Planes, trains, and automobiles were more likely to be the mode of transportation for most Americans in the Bicentennial year, however. According to industry sources, eighty-six million Americans would take some kind of Bicentennial trip, and 1976 was expected to set a record for travel. Vacations were longer in 1976, and gasoline prices had gone down since the peak of the energy crisis a few years back. (Regular gas cost an average fifty-five cents per gallon.) As well, there were more fuel-efficient cars on the road (an increasing number of them made in Japan), making many Americans eager to jump in their cars to go somewhere that sounded interesting or fun.[317]

Mystic Seaport, Connecticut, was both, especially in 1976. As a nice alternative to all the colonial-era activities taking place, Mystic was focusing on the 1876 Centennial for the Bicentennial. Mystic was a thriving whaling and shipbuilding town in 1876, and visitors a century later would have the chance to relive those days in a variety of ways. Circa 1876 American flags were strewn throughout the town, and there were games, relay races, and military drills from the period. The very same patriotic sermon that had been delivered in Mystic in 1876 would be repeated word for word and sea chanties sung at the town's maritime museum. A highlight would be the arrival of the Gloucester fishing schooner *L.A. Dunton*, retrieved from the Seaport's old shipyard.[318]

Nautical life was one of a number of key themes of American history to be seen on new stamps and envelopes issued by the USPS in celebration of the Bicentennial. From late 1975 through 1976, the postal service introduced thirteen-cent embossed envelopes featuring the Seafaring Tradition, the American Homemaker, the American Farmer, the American Doctor, and the American Craftsman.[319] In addition to those, there was a Declaration of Independence strip of four thirteen-cent stamps, and the Bureau of the Mint was busy selling its Bicentennial coin sets and some commemorative medals.[320]

Those stamps and coins were being saved as collectibles not just by American philatelists and numismatists but by foreigners visiting the United States for the Bicentennial. In 1976, 1.5 million foreigners were expected to visit the United States because of the Bicentennial, but most planned to see other sites while they made the trip. (Disney World, New Orleans, and San Francisco were at the top of the list.) Some had moved a planned vacation up or back to coincide with the Bicentennial. The event was thus serving much like a world's fair or Olympics in that people from across the globe were mingling due to a common interest.[321]

Operation Sail was especially serving as a means of bringing people from different nations together. By June 1976, there were twenty-eight nations taking part, although the United States had far and away the greatest number of ships. (Of the 225 vessels, 62 were American, with England a very distant second at 13.) The ships reached Newport, Rhode Island, on June 26 and would leave for New York on July 1. From there it was on to Boston, after which the flotilla would split up to different ports of call.[322]

Some pundits viewed the international aspects of the Bicentennial as something that could be a positive force, both at home and abroad. With the tragedy of the Vietnam War still fresh in Americans' minds, a refresher course in the country's historical role in international relations could be especially helpful. "Perhaps the most valuable lesson which the Bicentennial can impart to foreign policy is that world leadership is not a possession which can be inherited, but a privilege, for which every generation must strive anew," believed Felix Gilbert, another Princeton professor.[323]

The Bicentennial could have been seen by leaders of foreign nation as typical American boosterism, but that was generally not the case. "Commemorating the U.S. Birthday is practically a worldwide event," noted *Time* magazine, with congratulations coming in not just from our allies but from Communist states in Eastern Europe. Some of Europe's royalty were heading to Washington to join the celebration with President Ford and the first lady, including Queen Elizabeth II, Monaco's Prince Rainier and Princess Grace, Spain's King Juan Carlos, and French President Valéry Giscard d'Estaing. Britain had loaned out a copy of the Magna Carta, a gesture that could be taken that there were no hard feelings for the events of a couple centuries back.[324]

President and Mrs. Ford and Queen Elizabeth II and Prince Philip on the Truman Balcony following the queen's official welcome at the White House.

Pope Paul did not attend the Bicentennial gala held at the White House, but he did send a "Bicentennial message" via the National Conference of Catholic Bishops from the Vatican. The Pope lauded American Catholics for their "sustained piety and generosity," especially the efforts to combat poverty in the United States and provide help to the needy in other lands. He also reaffirmed the church's position on abortion and euthanasia in a three-thousand-word message. Still, the Pope called for American Catholics to practice an "increased holiness of life," something that no doubt resonated with the more conservative.[325]

The opportunity for a local delegation like this one from Fort Lauderdale, Florida, to present a Bicentennial artifact in person to President Ford at the White House was quite an honor.

Conservatives in particular viewed the Bicentennial as an ideal opportunity to reflect on the nation's achievements and anticipate what may lie ahead. "This Bicentennial celebration of the birth of the United States of America is more than a parade of our national past," wrote President Gerald Ford in *Saturday Evening*

Post, "it is a preview of our future." That magazine had devoted a special issue to the Bicentennial in July/August 1976, and who better than the president of the United States to comment on the two hundredth anniversary of the Declaration of Independence? In addition to the usual flag waving, Ford (or his speechwriter) could not resist doing a little politicking in his brief message. "The independence for which every American yearns…is the unfinished business of our Bicentennial," he declared, drawing on classic Republican ideology as part of his ongoing battle to trim government bureaucracy and spending.[326]

A Culminating Moment

The day that millions of Americans were waiting for effectively began in Mars Hills, Maine, at 4:31 a.m. It was then that the "dawn's early light" reached the continental United States, something that usually went unnoticed in the easternmost town. But on July 4, 1976, the sunrise was acknowledged by the raising of a flag, a ceremony that was nationally televised. Meanwhile, across the United States and part of Canada, more than ten groups of mountain climbers were spending their July 4 by attempting to ascend Mount McKinley, the tallest peak in North America. The incongruence between these two happenings symbolized the disparate ways that Americans spent the long-anticipated day.[327]

Waiting as long as he could, Ford (with Warner tagging along) had decided to spend July 4 in a number of places. After a church service, Ford would go to Valley Forge to see the wagon train, then head to Philadelphia for its celebration at Independence Hall, on to New York City for the tall ships, and end the day in the

President Ford and a child waving from the Michigan wagon at the Bicentennial Wagon Train Pilgrimage encampment at Valley Forge State Park in Pennsylvania.

President Ford speaking at Independence Hall in Philadelphia on July 4, 1976.

White House to see the spectacular fireworks from the "Truman balcony" in private with the first lady.

What was said to be the biggest fireworks show in American history on the grounds of the Washington Monument was everything planners had hoped for. A large crowd gathered in the afternoon to put out their chairs, coolers, and tents, hoping for a good view of the display. Meanwhile, thousands of supporters of the People Bicentennial Commission were making their presence known near the Jefferson Memorial, carrying banners with their motto, "Don't Tread on Me." They later marched to the Mall while chanting slogans such as "Mobil, Exxon, ITT, Down with Corporate Tyranny."[328]

President Ford and a dapper Warner commencing the ringing of Bicentennial bells across the nation while on the flight deck of the USS Forrestal during Operation Sail in New York Harbor.

The pyrotechnics in Washington, DC, were of course just a small part of how Americans spent their July 4 weekend. *Time* magazine described those few days as "a culminating moment of raucous blowout compounded of Disneyland pageantry and kitsch, perfervid oratory, sentiment, and sentimentality dissent." The variety of the goings-on were almost beyond description: Elton John performed in Boston decked out as the Statue of Liberty; three thousand Italian Americans in Rome, New York, consumed six hundred pounds of pasta along with six hundred pounds of sausage; and in Bartow, Florida, a 134th birthday party was held for former slave Charlie Smith, who was the oldest American and reportedly the only person who recalled the Centennial.[329]

Part of the very busy New York Harbor on July 4, 1976.

One of the many striking tall ships.

Naturalizing Americans was especially popular that weekend. In Chicago, 1,776 new citizens were sworn in, as were 7,000 in Miami. Marvin Rosenblum's "Hands Across America" never materialized, but there was a ten-mile stretch of linking on Chicago's South Side. Time capsules too were being buried across America. (One man in Seward, Nebraska, interred a 1975 Chevrolet Vega, a Kawasaki motorcycle, and his aquamarine leisure suit.)[330] Philadelphia was home to the biggest birthday cake ever made; the five-story thing, which was sponsored by Sara Lee, served 200,000. Sex workers in some cities were said to be offering "Bicentennial Specials," the price naturally being $17.76.[331]

New Philadelphia, meanwhile, which was in Ohio, had no Liberty Bell, but it did have one of the best hog-calling contests in the country. Residents of the town headed downtown over the July 4 weekend to hear the hollers, which were judged on the basis of "originality, volume of voice, and the ability of the hog to understand it." As it had done for the last dozen years, Elko, Nevada, was having its National Basque Festival, in which competitors were judged by how far they could walk with a 175-pound cement block in each hand. (The sport had been brought to this country by Basques who had settled in Nevada to become sheepherders in the late nineteenth century.) And in Pago Pago, Tutuila, American Samoans would celebrate *tutoatasi* ("independence" in Samoan), both the country's and their own as a U.S. protectorate, with traditional activities such as coconut cutting, outrigger canoe races, and spear throwing.[332]

There seemed to be no limit to the reports coming into news services regarding how Americans would be spending their Bicentennial weekend. The Battle of Pearl Harbor was being reenacted—but in Colorado Springs rather than Hawaii—by a

A 1974 re-creation of a historical event in Alexandria, Virginia, one of many held across the country.

President Ford addressing one hundred brand-new American citizens in a Bicentennial naturalization ceremony at Monticello, the historic home of Thomas Jefferson, in Charlottesville, Virginia, on July 5, 1976.

group calling themselves the Confederate Air Force. In Carnegie, Oklahoma, a Kiowa Tribe would hold two days of prayer, engage in "Gourd Clan" dances, and exchange gifts in a sacred circle. Last, but hardly least, there would be another signing of the Declaration of Independence, this one in Tell City, Indiana, with a Methodist minister playing Thomas Jefferson, a department store manager performing as Sam Adams, and a retired judge in the role of John Hancock.[333]

The United States was not the only country observing the Bicentennial, however. Israel had created a one-thousand-acre Bicentennial Park, while the Revere Bell was put on display in Singapore. (The bell had been presented to a cathedral in 1843 by the wife of the first U.S. Consul in Singapore.) France was recognizing the event in a variety of ways, including the release of a special Moet & Chandon Bicentennial Champagne and a Hennessey cognac. Rodeos in Dusseldorf and rock concerts in Berlin were a couple of tributes to the American Bicentennial in Germany, another being a cinematic reenactment of the role that Hessian mercenaries had played in the Revolutionary War. The Bicentennial was hugely popular in Japan; one cross-cultural enterprise was a *Viva America* floorshow featuring topless dancers brought over from Las Vegas especially for the occasion.[334] Unrelated, presumably, the people of Japan had gifted the United States fifty-three bonsai trees for the Bicentennial, which were installed at the National Arboretum in Washington for public viewing.[335]

Such Bicentennial gaiety was short-lived, however. Almost as soon as the last sparkler fizzled out in early July, in fact, many Americans wondered what lay in store for the remainder of 1976. The year was only halfway over, after all, meaning there could potentially be a lot more celebrating in the "Bicentennial Year." If history was any judge, however, there wouldn't be. "Remarkably little was said or remembered about America's Centennial celebration," *Time* observed a week after July 4, with minimal festivities held after the Philadelphia exposition shut down on November 10, 1876, after its six-month run.[336]

Some took the time to digest the Bicentennial blur of the last few years, especially its climax the first week of July. "I don't know about you, but I'm still trying to sort out a kaleidoscope of bicentennial day impressions before they dissolve," wrote John Beaufort of the *Christian Science Monitor* on July 15, feeling there was "a once-in-a-lifetime sense of national unity." Equally memorable for Beaufort, however, was "the crazy-quilt, jig-saw variety of it all," he explained, summarizing this hodgepodge as "the American collage."[337]

For President Ford, it was precisely that sense of national unity that left the man on an emotional high for days after July 4. "It was the feeling of people together," he said to a staff member, adding that, "Something wonderful happened to America this past weekend." His administration was wondering how that high that many Americans were feeling could be extended through November, when Ford would run for reelection. The international goodwill generated from the Bicentennial could be worth billions of defense dollars, some were saying, another reason why the challenge-riddled event ultimately paid off.[338]

Not everyone felt the Bicentennial was a wonderful experience, however. Vernon Jordan, who had consistently voiced his displeasure about how the event was unfolding, reiterated that view a few weeks after July 4. The country missed an opportunity to take a hard look at itself, especially with regard to race relations, he stated. "A proper Bicentennial observance would re-examine the ideals that led to the founding of this nation and the gap between those ideals and the reality of today," Jordan wrote in the *Baltimore Afro-American*. Rather than hold a useful debate that could lay the foundation for the next one hundred years, the country waved flags, sang patriotic songs, lit firecrackers, and bought a great deal of stuff that would be prime fodder for yard sales very soon.[339]

Others felt that given the Bicentennial's focus on the origins and history of the nation, the event could have served as an excellent platform by which to determine how to advance the well-being of all citizens. "The most meaningful celebration of the Bicentennial would be to apply to current conditions the democratic and liberating principles this country was founded on," Alvin Kogut of Adelphi University contended in the journal *Social Work*. Kogut agreed with Jeremy Rifkin that corporations were the new Tories and that an overhaul of the political and economic system was in order to give power back to the people. Couldn't the Bicentennial have started that process, or at least its discussion, he wondered?[340]

Parting Ways

It was, perhaps more than anyone else, Philadelphians who were asking that question. Millions of dollars had been spent by the city over the years on planning for the Bicentennial, and precious few residents were happy with how it had turned out. (The idea for some kind of celebration in Philadelphia actually predated discussion of such in Congress by quite a few years. Way back in September 1957, then Mayor Richardson Dilworth asked the Junior Chamber of Commerce to come up with some kind of plan for 1976.) Fewer than 10 percent of the forecasted twenty million visitors had come to Philadelphia for its celebrations, however, making the event a bust for the business community. The Legionnaire's disease outbreak in late July 1976 had further dampened tourists' desire to visit the City of Brotherly Love in late summer and fall.[341]

A much different scenario for Philadelphia's Bicentennial could have played out that in retrospect would have been far more sanguine. It had been proposed that instead of a world's fair or another major project that available funds be used for housing the poor, more hospitals and daycare centers, better public schools, or for much needed improvements to municipal services, particularly those that would benefit the African American community. None of that had happened, of course, and there was little to show for all the money that had been spent.[342]

Such reflections on the Bicentennial quickly faded after the climactic July 4 weekend, however. Cuts to the 180 or so staff members of the ARBA were made in August, the beginning of its dissolution, which would be complete in a year (by law). More employees would be laid off in October, as there would be little need for the historians, publicity personnel, and computer specialists that made up the staff. The main tasks of the ARBA were now completion of a final report on the Bicentennial for Congress and the boxing up of materials, files, and equipment to be sent to either the National Archives or the Interior Department. Career federal workers who were on loan to the ARBA from other agencies were hoping to get their old jobs back while the new hires were already looking around Washington for work.[343]

Another sign that the Bicentennial was fast becoming a memory was the half-price discounting of souvenirs in retail shops that had carried them. Sales of the items were less than store owners had hoped, even those that had borne the ARBA symbol. The cheaper, nonofficial stuff had actually sold better than the authorized products, the latter of which consumers felt was overpriced. Some real bargains could now be had for those wanting something by which to remember the Bicentennial. At Woodward & Lothrop, a Washington, DC department store, for example, women's underpants adorned with a fife and drum, illustration of Paul Revere's ride, or the Declaration of Independence was priced at just $1.35.[344]

A major contributor to the disappointing souvenir sales was the lower-than-expected number of tourists in many areas. In Vermont, for example, tourist "inflow" was in 1976 about the same as in 1975, which had not been a great year. Business owners felt that local officials and the media had scared people away with their predictions of crowds that would overwhelm the roads and hotels. As well, the fact that the Bicentennial had largely turned out to be a "mosaic" of thousands of hometown celebrations had kept the tourist count down in New England, even as the Summer Olympics were taking place in Montreal (just seventy miles north of the border of Vermont).[345]

Hoteliers in Philadelphia, many of whom had invested in upgrading their accommodations, were especially disappointed with the no-shows. Many tourists did come to the city for the celebrations, particularly those at Independence Hall, but most had jumped back in their cars and didn't stay overnight. The upstaging of Philadelphia by New York's Operation Sail was another factor in innkeepers' displeasure in Bicentennial business. Mayor Frank Rizzo had vigorously appealed to the White House for fifteen thousand armed National Guard troops to be brought in to handle the crowds and possible violence (to no avail), but there had been no such domestic emergency.[346]

Federal Reserve Bank officials were less than pleased about the results of what was perhaps their biggest contribution to the Bicentennial—the $2 bill. The bills had been reintroduced into circulation in April 1976 as a tribute to the past but had been a bust, as Americans simply didn't want them. Much to the chagrin of the Federal Reserve, 2,250,000 $2 bills had been issued, but most of them were sitting in banks' cash drawers. It cost the same to print a $1 bill and a $2 bill, so there would have been significant savings in printing costs had Americans taken to the bills bearing Jefferson's likeness rather than stick to their Washingtons.[347]

With all this griping, much of it financial in nature, one had to wonder if anything enduring would result from the Bicentennial. The "feeling of people together," as President Ford had put it, would no doubt soon fade as Americans focused on more pressing matters, like paying their bills. If one had to choose one positive that appeared to have longevity, a good case could be made for a greater interest in and respect for history. This was much the same as in 1876 when Americans celebrated its Centennial, as a U.S. Bureau of Education report documented at the time:

> *The centennial commemorations are quickening the historical spirit. Anniversaries of battles or other important events in our national history are increasing in frequency. Orations and newspapers are full of history. We may expect histories, national and local, already published to be revised; and records of families, societies, churches, institutions, towns, and states to be searched out, studied, and published.* [348]

A century later, a similar thing appeared to be taking place even as the festivities of the Bicentennial grew faint. Professional historians may have remained dubious about some of the forms of telling of the past employed, but the sheer volume of history produced over the past few years was impressive. "We have all been subjected to hours (as well as a host of 'Bicentennial minutes') of history celebrating our nation's past," John Berry noted in *Library Journal* in November 1976, thinking that it had provided useful lessons for both the present and the future.[349]

More attention was notably being paid to African American history, especially during colonial days in New England. "The Bicentennial in New England is the occasion for a thorough re-examination of history as now taught and written," observed Georgia E. Ireland of the *New York Amsterdam News*, stating that this reappraisal was "resulting in a new assessment of the role played by Black men and women in the struggle for independence." Lectures, books, monuments, and museums were the results of research into the mostly neglected area, for Ireland "a legacy of the Bicentennial commemoration." Boston, New Haven, Connecticut, and Rhode Island were just a few of the places where local Bicentennial commissions were working with historians to learn more about Blacks' contribution to the birth of the nation.[350]

The Bicentennial was also an opportune time to learn more about the Parting Ways settlement in Plymouth, Massachusetts; the ninety-four-acre tract had been deeded to four enslaved Black men, Cato Howe, Prince William, Plato Turner, and Quamany. The men were freed on the basis of their brave soldiering in the Revolutionary War, the beginnings of what was believed to be the country's first Black settlement. After seeing those men's graves at Parting Ways, Marjorie Anderson, president of the Plymouth Bicentennial Advisory Committee on Black History and Culture (and a member of the state and local Bicentennial Committees), was leading the way to create a museum, library, and research center.[351] (A historical interpretive display exists at the site today.)[352]

Another cemetery on Long Island was contributing to African American history because of the Bicentennial. Little had been known about Old Burying Ground near Wantagh and North Bellmore before 1976, but Karl F. Heiffer changed that after he wrote a booklet about it. The area, which had been known as "The Brush," had been inhabited by descendants of slaves who had been freed around the time of the Revolutionary War. Some of those buried there were Civil War soldiers who had served in Black units. The Bicentennial had been the impetus for local patriotic groups and the towns to place historical markers at Old Burying Ground that told its fascinating story. Heiffer's booklet was also distributed to schools, libraries, and museums at no cost, offering many an education that would not have been possible.[353]

What Did It All Mean?

Filling in the large gaps of the nation's past was undoubtedly one of the key legacies of the Bicentennial, which would itself soon be considered history. The official end of the Bicentennial had originally been slated for 1981—the two hundredth anniversary of the Battle of Yorktown. (Some had made a case for 1983, the anniversary of the relinquishing of New York by the British.) By December 1976, however, Americans, well known for their interest in what's next, had tired of the Bicentennial, and were ready to move on. "December 31, 1976, for all intents and purposes, will mark the end of the national birthday party that has been losing its champagne fizz since July 4," the *Atlanta Constitution* made note.[354]

Indeed, nine of the ten regional Bicentennial administrations had closed (only Denver remained open), and the ARBA would shut down in June 1977, with any lingering business handled

A small portion of the handmade crafts sent to the White House.

by the Department of the Interior. The head of the ARBA, John Warner, had retired his post effective September 30, but the man was hardly idle, having recently become the husband of Elizabeth Taylor (her seventh). Some Bicentennial commemorations spilled into 1977, however. George Washington's midnight crossing of the Delaware River would be reenacted on December 25 (the boat regretfully had to be towed), but New Jersey planned to carry on for an additional ten days to honor the first and second Battles of Trenton and the Battle of Princeton. As well, a handful of projects, including "The World of Franklin and Jefferson," "Remember the Ladies," "Amistad II," "Man and His Development," and the Freedom Train journey would cross over into 1977.[355]

Despite all the criticism that had been directed at it and its predecessor, an audit of the ARBA's achievements was impressive. Over the course of Warner's sixteen-month tenure, the ARBA orchestrated 65,000 projects in 12,566 communities, doling out $28 million in grants and matching funds to states and territories. Remarkably, given how cash poor it had been for most its existence, the ARBA was giving back $971,000 to the U.S. Treasury, having turned a profit from its product licensing and other ventures.[356] The People's Bicentennial Commission, meanwhile, announced that there had been 105,000 attendees at its three major demonstrations and that 20,000 people became official members of the group. While the ARBA was no more, Rifkin's organization planned to continue on as the People's Business Commission, whose mission was to "democratize wealth and power."[357]

In the final days of 1976, many Americans looked back on the "Bicentennial year" to provide context to what had been an extraordinary event in the history of the nation. Most of the remaining Bicentennial products in shops were now in clearance bins along with Christmas items that hadn't sold, a rather depressing sight. Each town in America had celebrated the Bicentennial in its own way, but there were common themes—a stirring July 4 parade, the formation of a local historical association, and perhaps a colonial fair featuring a reenactment of Paul Revere's ride. Some older communities had gone further by taking a survey of their historic buildings and trying to get them listed in the National Register of Historic Places. Historians, particularly those specializing in the American colonial era, were happy to have their usually not wildly popular field put in the spotlight. Enrollment in college courses in the subject was up, and publishers were more receptive to manuscripts covering some aspect of the topic.[358]

When asked whether the Bicentennial was a success, Americans not surprisingly answered quite differently. Some felt much like President Ford, believing that the event was a wonderful and rare occasion to collectively view the nation at its best. "It really made everyone aware of what we are and what we should be," said one woman from Port Jefferson Station on Long Island. Even though his job as New York State historian was ironically eliminated in 1976 due to budget cuts, Louis Tucker believed that the Bicentennial was a virtual godsend. "We had a period of Americans being really down in the dumps," he told *Newsday*, defining that stretch of time as running between the early years of the Vietnam War to Watergate. "It was almost providential that the Bicentennial came at just that precise time," he added, as the event offered "a chance to lift our heads up and swell with a little bit of pride."[359]

Hard data backed up Tucker's claim that Americans had been down in the dumps due to actions taken by the federal government. A 1976 study conducted by the Public Agenda Foundation confirmed that many Americans believed that moral leadership in government had been strongly lacking. Respondents cited political corruption, unfair public policies, a lack of respect for the law, and a general sense of aimlessness and loss of purpose as reasons why so many felt despondent.[360]

Others, however, thought that the Bicentennial was a singular flop that had been engulfed by excess commercialism. This contingent was glad that the event that had been in the making for a decade was finally over. Children were not sure to make of the Bicentennial, fully appreciative of the July 4 fireworks but not quite understanding why so much had been made of it. (Younger children were apt to think the celebration had been a birthday for George Washington or some other Founding Father.)[361]

While the vast majority of retailers were disappointed that Bicentennial products had not moved off their shelves as hoped, some marketers were delighted to look at their 1976 balance sheets. The country's biggest maker of flags, the Oaks, Pennsylvania–based Dettra Flag Company, reported that it had sold hundreds of thousands of the Stars and Stripes ranging in price from $0.90 to $500. (The company's factory had to hire a night shift for the first time in its seventy-five-year history to produce that many flags, some of which are likely still flying.) Executives at the Bradley Time Company were similarly tickled pink, as the company had sold tens of thousands of its Freedom Ringer alarm clock. The clock, which sold for $23.95, featured two miniature Minute Men flanking a Liberty Bell that sat on top of the Declaration of Independence.[362]

Having the last say, at least in this story, was an editor for the *Christian Science Monitor*, a publication that before the advent of *USA Today* served as the principal national newspaper. "What did it all mean?" the anonymous editor asked readers, the answer being "nothing" unless the real reasons for the celebration were understood and carried forward. It had become rather corny to glorify the phrase "life, liberty, and the pursuit of happiness," but those words were remarkable not just in their time but today. The promise of democracy had spread around the world, as colony after colony rejected imperialism for independence as America had done two centuries ago, and it was this powerful, humanistic movement that the Bicentennial symbolized.[363]

Almost as important, however, the Bicentennial had also operated on a local level, as this editor made clear:

> *Along with the schlock there were the school students painting bicentennial walls along their small-town railroad track; the church members throwing their amateur talents into a civic show of patriotism and religion; the thousand-and-one small and large events in which Americans made gestures in honor of their heritage.* [364]

The American Bicentennial was over, but the experience would not be forgotten.

A Bicentennial edition flag in Hurley, New York.

Epilogue

The benefit of time allows us to place the American Bicentennial in useful context and perspective. A half century after the event, we have a better understanding of what it meant and its place in American history. Arriving at a critical moment in our history, the Bicentennial offered Americans a welcome diversion from all the troubles of the day. Reminding Americans of their literally revolutionary past revived a sense of togetherness when the country was fragmenting in all sorts of directions. Patriotism was hardly the order of the day, but the steady stream of red, white, and blue seeped into the national consciousness, creating an unparalleled sense of unity and pride.

While there was no shortage of skeptics and critics, especially as related to the inevitable commercialism that permeated the event, the Bicentennial largely achieved its objective of enlightening Americans that despite our many differences, we remained a single people. A reasonable case can be made that the event served to improve Americans' general frame of mind and lit a kind of cultural spark that would accelerate in the latter part of the 1970s. The realization of positive and enduring social reforms would have been the best outcome of the Bicentennial, but one could argue that the event foreshadowed the patriotic spirit and bullish economy of the Reagan era.

The American Bicentennial also further exposed the deep flaws in our rhetorical democracy and our consumerist way of life. The greatest tension in the story was no doubt African Americans' ambivalence and downright antipathy toward the Bicentennial, a natural result of the racism so woven into the nation's past and the discrimination that people of color confronted in the 1970s on a daily basis. Like the world wars, the Bicentennial acted as a powerful force in African Americans' complex negotiation between their national and racial identities, creating a conversation that I believe the country needed to have. While there was no resolution (nor could there be), the issues raised helped bring "the American dilemma" into the national conversation that could have otherwise been manifested in much more negative ways.

The "Bicentennial year" ended in 1976, but the event trickled over into 1977. On January 7, President Ford delivered the last of CBS's Bicentennial Minutes (which had won an Emmy Award). "It was a time to take a fresh look at our past and move forward together into our future," the president said, as good as any way to describe the Bicentennial in a single sentence. An amazing array of personalities had preceded Ford in narrating Bicentennial Minutes, including government officials (e.g., Shirley Chisholm), military men (e.g., General Omar Bradley), physicians (e.g., Dr. Lee Salk), writers (e.g., Tennessee Williams), actors (e.g., Paul Newman), and a few unexpected guests (e.g., Alfred Hitchcock). As a time capsule of a certain time and place, these minutes form an intriguing and valuable body of work that warrant further study.[365]

As the dust of the Bicentennial settled, Americans weighed the event's pros and cons, particularly as related to the number of people who participated in some way. Managers of popular historical sites such as Colonial Williamsburg in Virginia, Independence Square in Philadelphia, and Old Sturbridge Village in Massachusetts were unequivocally disappointed with their turnout. The 1976 predictions for these and other destinations were way overblown, as many families avoided them in fear of being swamped by hordes of other visitors. The preceding year had been good for certain places, as some families chose to beat the crowds, and managers were hoping for a similar post-Bicentennial effect in 1977.[366]

Much of the media took time to offer their general assessment of the Bicentennial in early 1977. The *New Yorker* magazine, known for its rather snarky attitude toward anything populist, for example, offered its take, beginning in typical fashion. "The Bicentennial started out interesting, became tedious, became really tedious, and then continued past any considerations of whether it was interesting or not," an editor predictably quipped. Surprisingly, however, the magazine came around to the idea that with the event, the country was "involved in something basically good." "For our part, we liked the Bicentennial," the editor wrote, as "it left us with a tremendous clean-windshield feeling."[367]

Life, not surprisingly, glowingly praised how, as the headline of that magazine's summary of the Bicentennial went, "we proudly hailed a most glorious 4th." In a classic photographic essay, *Life* showed how the last Independence Day was "clearly grander and more glorious than ever." Cleverly, the magazine's editors invited readers to submit their own photos capturing the day's events with the best to be published; the contest generated no fewer than 5,575 entrants. Winners had recorded images of a stilt-walking Uncle Sam in Plainfield, Vermont; fireworks exploding over the

Statue of Liberty; a twentieth-century Minuteman in Boston; a Bicentennial wedding on Bainbridge Island, Washington; and skydivers in St. Louis.[368]

The National Urban League was far less complimentary, labeling the Bicentennial an out and out "bust" in economic terms for people of color. Joblessness among African Americans had risen in 1976, the organization reported, far more so than for Whites. "Many black communities today are economic disaster areas in need of urgent and substantial Federal aid," the league stated in March 1977, reaffirming its contention that the millions of dollars spent by the government on the Bicentennial could and should have been used in a different way than holding a giant birthday party.[369]

Indeed, many Americans questioned the wisdom of elected officials in how the latter had spent taxpayer money on the Bicentennial. It was true that thousands of communities across the country had celebrated the event in some way (Liberty Tree plantings were especially popular), with a couple of them truly spectacular. The tall ships sailing into New York Harbor was an unforgettable memory for those who had seen it on television or in person, as was the collection of covered wagons that converged in Valley Forge.[370]

But even these moments fell well short of what the Bicentennial perhaps should have been—an opportunity to launch much-needed social reforms. While all the parades and fireworks were certainly entertaining, couldn't we have accomplished something more substantive and enduring that would have somehow improved the lives of the American people? some reasonably asked. A fair number of taxpayers complained about the $50 million the administration had spent on the event, unhappy that their hard-earned money had gone toward frivolity during some tough economic times. (To be fair, corporations, other organizations, and state and local governments also picked up some of the tab.)[371]

John Warner, who had headed up the Bicentennial for two (Nixon and Ford) administrations, dismissed such criticism. "Admittedly, the Bicentennial failed to meet the expectations of some…but it rekindled the 'can do' spirit that has been the fiber and strength of this nation," he wrote in April 1977, proud of the giant party that had been thrown. Americans had regained some of the swagger that had been lost in the late 1960s and early 1970s, he felt; the grand celebration of the nation's past was reason to be optimistic about the future. Reeling from Vietnam, Watergate, the energy crisis, and dreaded "stagflation," the country needed a reason to be hopeful, Warner insisted, and the Bicentennial proved to be just that. "It is my belief that the Bicentennial mark[ed] a major turning point for the United States of America and its people," he declared, thinking the nation had been not just "rediscovered" but "born again."[372]

Warner had left the all-but-defunct ARBA in September 1976, making it his replacement's job to permanently shut down the agency. In doing so, acting administrator Jean McKee sent a letter to President Carter along with a draft of the ARBA's final report that Congress had required. Perhaps hoping to keep her job for a while longer, McKee urged the president to consider that the Bicentennial of the U.S. Constitution be recognized in 1987. (The Constitution was drafted in 1787 in the very same room where the Declaration of Independence had been written.) "That great document represents the beginning, not the end, of the creative process which brought into being the United States of America," the draft report read, going on to recommend that the two hundredth anniversary of the Constitution should be celebrated in some way.[373] Was America ready to have another colossal party in just ten years?

Apparently not, as the two hundredth anniversary of the Constitution in 1987 came and went with relatively little fanfare. (A three-day festival over Memorial Day weekend called "All Roads Lead to Philadelphia" was held in that city, but there was no nationwide celebration.)[374]

But America will get another chance with the upcoming Semiquincentennial, the 250th anniversary of the signing of the Declaration of Independence, through July 2026. Celebrations in many cities, including Philadelphia, Boston, New York City, Louisville, Pittsburgh, Charleston, and Denver are currently in the works. Many activities (not the least of which is learning how to pronounce *Semiquincentennial* (or quarter millennial) are planned in Philadelphia, including the Young People's Continental Congress ("a youth-focused event bringing together delegates from across the country to explore the themes of democracy and to engage in civic dialogue"); the 250th birthdays of the U.S. Navy and Marine Corps; *The Declaration's Journey* (a special exhibition exploring the history and global impact of the Declaration of Independence from 1776 to today at the Museum of the American Revolution); rounds one and two of the NCAA Division I Men's Basketball Tournament; FIFA World Cup 26; and the 2026 Major League Baseball All-Star Game.[375]

Sounds like a wonderful celebration, no doubt, but for myself nothing can compare to the Bicentennial, as America is a much different place than it was in 1976 and Americans a much different people.

Notes

Introduction

1. Linda P. Gross and Theresa R. Snyder, *Philadelphia's 1876 Centennial Exhibition* (*Arcadia, 2005*), *7*. See also Bruno Gilberti, *Designing the Centennial: A History of the 1876 International Exhibition in Philadelphia* (University Press of Kentucky, 2021).
2. Robert Hartje, "Celebrating the Bicentennial: 'Lessons' from Past Centennials," *The Historian*, May 1975, 394.
3. For a small sample of the many books about the Bicentennial published at the time, see Richard B. Morris, ed., *The American Revolution, 1763–1783: A Bicentennial Collection* (University of South Carolina Press, 1971); *A Bicentennial Portrait of the American People* (U.S. News & World Report Books, 1975); Calvin D. Linton, ed., *The Bicentennial Almanac:1886–1976; 200 Years of America* (Thomas Nelson, 1975); and Sol Stember, *The Bicentennial Guide to the American Revolution* (New York: E.P. Dutton, 1976).
4. Tammy S. Gordon, *The Spirit of 1976: Commerce, Community, and the Politics of Commemoration* (University of Massachusetts Press, 2013).
5. For more on the history of the Bicentennial and, more generally, the ways in which Americans from all walks of life recognized the nation's past, see M.J. Rymsza-Pawlowska, *History Comes Alive: Public History and Popular Culture in the 1970s* (University of North Carolina Press, 2017) and Christopher Capozzola's chapter "It Makes You Want to Believe in the Country," in *America in the Seventies*, edited

by Beth Bailey and David Farber (University Press of Kansas, 2004). Also quite valuable is John Bodnar's *Remaking America: Public Memory, Commemoration, and Patriotism in the Twentieth Century* (Princeton University Press, 1991).

6. Lawrence R. Samuel, *Pledging Allegiance: American Identity and the Bond Drive of World War II* (Smithsonian Institution Press, 1997).
7. Lawrence R. Samuel, *The End of the Innocence: The 1964–1965 New York World's Fair* (Syracuse University Press, 2007).
8. Margot Hornblower, "Bicentennial Ripoff Charges Deplored," *Washington Post*, February 8, 1976, 3.
9. "Foreman, Frazier Put on Bicentennial Garb for Plugs," *Jet*, June 17, 1976, 56.

Chapter 1

10. Bradillac, "COAL: 1972 Ford Mustang Sprint Special Edition—'What's Red, White, And Blue And Brand New From Ford?,'" Curbside Classic, March 24, 2024, https://www.curbsideclassic.com/cars-of-a-lifetime/coal-1972-ford-mustang-sprint-special-edition-whats-red-white-and-blue-and-brand-new-from-ford/; "Cars of the American Revolution," Palm Springs Automobilist, July 3, 2016, http://psautomobilist.blogspot.com/2016/07/cars-of-american-revolution.html. AMC was first in marketing red, white, and blue cars, and General Motors soon followed Ford.
11. Kenneth Boyd, "Oil Your Muskets for Bunker Hill!," *Washington Post*, March 20, 1965, A12.
12. Robert L. Asher, "Lone GOP Spark Struck in January Becomes a Johnson July 4th Special," *Washington Post*, June 30, 1966, B1.
13. Boyd, "Oil Your Muskets for Bunker Hill!"
14. Boyd, "Oil Your Muskets for Bunker Hill!"
15. "The National Bicentennial: 1975-76," *Bulletin of the American Academy of Arts and Sciences*, February 1966, 8–9.
16. "Revolution Anniversary Commission Requested," *Washington Post*, March 11, 1966, A8.
17. Carroll Kilpatrick, "President Looks Ahead to Our 200th Birthday," *Washington Post*, July 9, 1966, A2.
18. "Bicentennial Commission," *Washington Post*, July 17, 1966, E6.
19. Wolf Von Eckardt, "Mission '76': An Idea vs. Fireworks," *Washington Post*, April 20, 1969, 35.
20. Von Eckardt, "Mission '76.'"
21. Von Eckardt, "Mission '76.'"
22. Von Eckardt, "Mission '76.'"

23. "Who'll Host the '76 Fair," *Washington Post*, July 31, 1969, C2.
24. "New Jersey Enacts Bicentennial Bill," *History News*, August 1969, 166.
25. Ellen Hoffman, "D.C. Woos Bicentennial with $5 Billion Plan," *Washington Post*, September 25, 1969, B7.
26. "Library of Congress Bicentennial Office," *History News*, December 1969, 254.
27. "Series on '76," *Washington Post*, April 24, 1970, B10.
28. "Endowment Awards Grant to ASSLH for Study of Bicentennial Programs," *History News*, July 1970, 144.
29. Wolf Von Eckhardt, "After 200 Years, Is There a Spirit of '76,'" *Washington Post*, June 14, 1970, C3.
30. Wolf Von Eckhardt, "Bicentennial Seeks Spirit of '76," *Washington Post*, June 28, 1970, C3.
31. "...And Six Years from Today," *Washington Post*, July 4, 1970, 12.
32. "Bicentennial Head," *Washington Post*, August 7, 1970, C4.
33. Samuel, *End of the Innocence*.
34. "Philadelphia Chosen Official Revolution Bicentennial Center," *History News*, August 1970, 180.
35. Robert Hartje, "American Bicentennial," *History News*, September 1970, 194.
36. Len Lear, "Bicentennial Will Bulldoze Hundreds Out of Their Homes, Leader Charges," *Philadelphia Tribune*, February 17, 1970, 5; Pamela Haynes, "Spokesmen for Community Groups Criticize Bicentennial as Big Business Money Grab," *Philadelphia Tribune*, October 3, 1970.
37. "Philadelphians Seek More Voice in Bicentennial Plans," *Baltimore Afro-American*, May 2, 1970, 20; Len Lear, "Bicentennial Rapped at W. Phila. Conference on Area's Self-Determination," *Philadelphia Tribune*, December 19, 1970, 6.
38. Ethel L. Payne, "Will Blacks Help Mark 200 Years of Freedom?," *Chicago Daily Defender*, August 23, 1971, 8.
39. Payne, "Will Blacks Help Mark."
40. Payne, "Will Blacks Help Mark."
41. Leavitt F. Morris, "Preparing for U.S. Bicentennial," *Christian Science Monitor*, May 11, 1971, B8.
42. "Smithsonian Revolution Bicentennial Plan Features Inventory of American Paintings," *History News*, May 1971, 113.
43. Paul J.C. Friedlander, "Progress Report on U.S. Bicentennial," *New York Times*, May 9, 1971, XX59.
44. Friedlander, "Progress Report on U.S. Bicentennial."
45. Friedlander, "Progress Report on U.S. Bicentennial."
46. "Nixon 'Stealing the Revolution,'" *Washington Post*, August 13, 1971, B3.
47. "Nixon 'Stealing the Revolution.'"

48. "'76 Open House Planned in U.S.," *Christian Science Monitor*, September 9, 1971, 10.
49. "'76 Open House Planned in U.S."
50. William Greider, "Group Plans to Show Radical Spirit of '76," *Washington Post*, October 15, 1971, A3.
51. Eugene L. Meyer, "Bicentennial Ignoring Minorities—Mathias," *Washington Post*, December 5, 1971, E1.
52. "Women's Role in the Bicentennial," *Philadelphia Tribune*, May 6, 1972, 15.
53. "Bicentennial Ignoring Minorities."
54. "The Bicentennial: Where Is the Commitment," *Washington Post*, December 10, 1971, A26.
55. "Speedy Train Net Proposed for '76," *New York Times*, July 18, 1971, S24.
56. "Bicentennial Commission Notes Accomplishments," *Boston Globe*, December 9, 1971, 6.
57. "Scattered Anniversary," *Time*, June 12, 1972.
58. "Bicentennial: Too Old for a Birthday Party?," *New York Times*, May 21, 1972, E2.
59. "Parks Proposed for Bicentennial," *Christian Science Monitor*, February 24, 1972, 4.
60. Franklin R. Burns Jr., "'Craftsmen' for Bicentennial," *Washington Post*, April 2, 1972, C5.
61. Lance Carden, "Boston Bicentennial Plans Bloom," *Christian Science Monitor*, May 11, 1972, 10.
62. Carden, "Boston Bicentennial Plans."
63. Robert L. Turner, "Bicentennial World's Fair Rejected," *Washington Post*, May 17, 1972, A22.
64. "Bicentennial Celebration Should Be Next Order of Business," *Philadelphia Tribune*, May 20, 1972, 8.
65. Ellen Kaye, "The Philadelphia Story: Bye Bye Bicentennial," *Harper's Bazaar*, September 1972, 124–25.
66. Eugene L. Meyer, "The Big Birthday Bungle," *Washington Post*, July 2, 1972, C1.
67. Meyer, "Big Birthday Bungle."
68. Meyer, "Big Birthday Bungle."
69. Meyer, "Big Birthday Bungle."
70. "3 Negroes Named to the Revolution Commission," *Atlanta Daily World*, May 4, 1972, 13.
71. Meyer, "Big Birthday Bungle."
72. Ethel L. Payne, "Brothers Move Insures Black Roles in Fete," *Chicago Daily Defender*, August 24, 1971, 8.
73. Payne, "Brothers Move Insures Black Roles."

74. "Program Launched to Identify Black American History Sites," *Atlanta Daily World*, September 8, 1972, 8.
75. Carroll Kilpatrick, "Nixon Will Invite Visits by the World's People," *Washington Post*, July 5, 1972, A10.
76. "Letting Our Heritage Down," *Washington Post*, August 1, 1972, A18.
77. Eugene Meyer, "Study Raps Bicentennial Staff," *Washington Post*, July 20, 1972, A2.
78. "Letting Our Heritage Down."
79. Eugene Meyer, "Bicentennial Director Quits; Management Was Criticized," *Washington Post*, August 2, 1972, A8.
80. Eugene L. Meyer, "Indians Protest Bicentennial," *Washington Post*, August 3, 1972, A3.
81. Meyer, "Indians Protest Bicentennial."
82. Marlene Cimons, "Women's Role in U.S. Bicentennial," *Los Angeles Times*, August 6, 1972, C3.
83. Cimons, "Women's Role."
84. Cimons, "Women's Role in U.S. Bicentennial."
85. Eugene L. Meyer, "Bicentennial Commission: Deeply Involved in Politics," *Washington Post*, August 14, 1972, A1. With regard to how those documents were obtained, see Bob Arnebeck, "Expose of an Expose: Confessions of the Bicentennial Commission Spy," *Washington Post*, March 18, 1973, PC10.
86. Eugene L. Meyer, "Red, White, Blue—and Green," *Washington Post*, August 15, 1972, A1.
87. Meyer, "Red, White, Blue."
88. Eugene L. Meyer and Stephen Green, "Bicentennial Budget Bill Withdrawn," *Washington Post*, August 15, 1972, A1.
89. Eugene L. Meyer, "Diluting the Spirit of '76," *Washington Post*, August 16, 1972, A1.
90. "Boosting the Bicentennial," *Washington Post*, August 17, 1972, A18.
91. Eugene L. Meyer, "Sen. Pastore Quits Units on Bicentennial," *Washington Post*, August 17, 1972, B1.
92. Eugene L. Meyer, "Bicentennial 'Attacks' Decried by Republicans," *Washington Post*, August 19, 1972, E28.
93. Eugene L. Meyer, "Hill Blacks Assail Bicentennial Panel," *Washington Post*, August 24, 1972, C1.
94. Eugene L. Meyer, "Counter Bicentennial Group Seeks End of Exploitation," *Washington Post*, September 8, 1972, C3.
95. Eugene L. Meyer, "Bicentennial Commission Acts to Get Fund from Congress," *Washington Post*, September 9, 1972, A3.
96. Eugene L. Meyer, "Mahoney, Rifkin: A 'Summit' on Bicentennial," *Washington Post*, September 11, 1972, A8.

97. Eugene L. Meyer, "Probe of Bicentennial Commission Is Slated," *Washington Post*, September 13, 1972, B10.
98. Eugene L. Meyer, "Bicentennial Unit Limits Its Powers," *Washington Post*, October 21, 1972, B7.
99. Eugene L. Meyer, "Bicentennial Panel Wants Funds Doubled," *Washington Post*, December 12, 1972, A10.
100. Eugene L. Meyer, "Bicentennial Group Cuts Back Festivity," *Washington Post*, October 27, 1972, A4.
101. Eugene L. Meyer, "GAO Is Mildly Critical of Bicentennial Group," *Washington Post*, December 22, 1972, C14.
102. Eugene L. Meyer, "Bicentennial Commission Hit in Report by House Unit Staff," *Washington Post*, December 30, 1972, A3.

Chapter 2

103. Herb Brock, "Bicentennial License Tag Production Hits Snag," *Philadelphia Tribune*, December 13, 1973, B11.
104. Frederick B. Hill, "Blacks, Indians Urge Congress to Expand Scope of Bicentennial," *Baltimore Sun*, January 10, 1973, C13.
105. Eugene L. Meyer, "Nixon to Change Bicentennial Setup," *Washington Post*, February 1, 1973, A3.
106. "Marching Toward '76," *Washington Post*, February 9, 1973, A18.
107. Eugene Meyer, "House Panel Criticizes White House for Proposing a Bicentennial Czar," *Washington Post*, March 15, 1973, A28.
108. "March to Retrace Maine-Quebec Trek," *Christian Science Monitor*, March 17, 1973, 3.
109. "March to Retrace Maine-Quebec Trek."
110. Ralph Hubley, "New England Races Tourist Timetable," *Christian Science Monitor*, April 24, 1973, B1.
111. Stewart Dill, "New England Races Tourist Timetable," *Christian Science Monitor*, April 24, 1973, B2.
112. Stephen Silha, "Bicentennial to Begin This Year in Boston," *Christian Science Monitor*, April 24, 1973, B2.
113. Leavitt F. Morris, "Bicentennial Buds in Northern N.E.," *Christian Science Monitor*, April 24, 1973, B6.
114. Eugene Meyer, "Panel Leaves Nation Without '76 Celebration," *Washington Post*, May 16, 1973, A2.
115. Eugene Meyer, "More Staff Sought for '76 Plans," *Washington Post*, May 17, 1973, A2.
116. "Seven Wasted Years," *Washington Post*, May 22, 1973, A22.
117. "Stamps Commemorate Boston Tea Party," *Christian Science Monitor*, June 14, 1973, 14.

118. Eugene L. Meyer, "Watergate and the 'Spirit of '76,'" *Washington Post*, July 2, 1973, A22.
119. John D. Rockefeller III, "Of Anniversaries and Revolutions," *Vital Speeches of the Day*, July 15, 1973, 597–601.
120. S.I. Hayakawa, "The Good Old Days—You Can Have Them," *Saturday Evening Post*, January/February 1974, 42.
121. Susan Fogg, "Support Claimed Growing for People's Bicentennial," *Atlanta Constitution*, July 2, 1973, 10B.
122. Tom Donnelly, "The New! Improved! American Bicentennial Fleet," *Washington Post*, September 2, 1973, H1.
123. Donnelly, "New! Improved! American Bicentennial Fleet."
124. "AASLH Publishes Robert Hartje's Guide to Meaningful Bicentennial Programs," *History News*, September 1973, 193.
125. "AASLH Publishes Robert Hartje's Guide."
126. Paul J. Asciolla, "U.S. History Needs Overhaul," *Chicago Tribune*, September 5, 1973, 18.
127. "Brainstorming the Bicentennial," *History News*, October 1973, 223.
128. Mimi Mead, "The Undebunkable George Washington," *Christian Science Monitor*, November 23, 1973, 22.
129. Colin Stewart, "U.S. 200th Birthday: Some Roadblocks?," *Christian Science Monitor*, November 8, 1973, 1.
130. "Bicentennial Debated in Philadelphia," *Christian Science Monitor*, November 8, 1973, 4.
131. "Hymns Sought for 1976 Bicentennial," *Philadelphia Tribune*, December 13, 1973, B3.
132. Stephen Isaacs, "Boston Tea Party Restaged," *Washington Post*, December 17, 1973, A1.
133. "Bicentennial Unit Created by Nixon," *Washington Post*, December 12, 1973, B23.
134. "Mahoney, Bicentennial Chief, Quits," *Washington Post*, December 27, 1973, A5.
135. Lou Cannon, "Warner Is Named to Head '76 Agency," *Washington Post*, March 11, 1974, A3.
136. James J. Kilpatrick, "The Bicentennial Back on Course," *Hartford Courant*, June 11, 1974, 18.
137. Don McLeod, "Bicentennial Aim: Look at Heritage," *Atlanta Constitution*, June 30, 1974, 3B.
138. Cannon, "Warner Is Named to Head."
139. John Alexander, "The Largest Birthday Cake in the World," *Saturday Evening Post*, March 1974, 22–23.
140. Stephen Isaacs, "Boston Tea Party Restaged," *Washington Post*, December 17, 1973, A1.

141. Isaacs, "Boston Tea Party Restaged."
142. August Heckscher, "In a Glass Darkly," *Christian Science Monitor*, April 19, 1974, 17.
143. Heckscher, "In a Glass Darkly." See Charles Beard, *An Economic Interpretation of the Constitution* (Macmillan, 1913).
144. "Cheapening the Bicentennial," *Christian Science Monitor*, May 17, 1974, 22.
145. Leonard Sloane, "Reuss Hits Bicentennial Tie-Ins," *New York Times*, April 13, 1974, 37.
146. "Dialogue on National Issues to Be Part of Bicentennial," *Christian Science Monitor*, June 5, 1974, 3B.
147. "The 732 Steps," *Time*, June 24, 1974, 71.
148. William H. Stringer, "America: Founding and Future," *Christian Science Monitor*, July 5, 1974, 16.
149. Ralph Hubley, "7 Ports Await? Bicentennial," *Christian Science Monitor*, July 9, 1974, 10.
150. Stringer, "America."
151. Stringer, "America."
152. Phil Casey, "On Reviving the $2 Bill," *Washington Post*, July 31, 1974, B1.
153. "Smithsonian Readies First Bicentennial Traveling Exhibit," *History News*, July 1974, 153.
154. "Brainstorming the Bicentennial," *History News*, July 1974, 155.
155. Harry Hoffman, "Philadelphia Bicentennial: Fort Mifflin Volunteers Are Ready for '76," *Christian Science Monitor*, October 15, 1974, B5.
156. "The Bicentennial Opportunity," *Washington Post*, August 5, 1974, A26.
157. Curtis J. Sitomer, "Leadoff Bicentennial Event—Pacific Fair in Los Angeles," *Christian Science Monitor*, August 9, 1974, 4.
158. Wolf Von Eckhardt, "Hucksterism, Kitsch, and the Promoting of the Buy-Centennial," *Washington Post*, August 17, 1974, B1.
159. Von Eckhardt, "Hucksterism, Kitsch."
160. Von Eckhardt, "Hucksterism, Kitsch."
161. "The Licensing of the Revolution," *Washington Post*, August 28, 1974, D5.
162. Von Eckhardt, "Hucksterism, Kitsch."
163. James L. Walker, "Eastward Ho! For '76 Wagon Train," *Christian Science Monitor*, August 22, 1974, 16; Margot Hornblower, "A Plan to Draw Up the Wagons in D.C.," *Washington Post*, November 24, 1974, A1.
164. Monty Hoyt, "Cross-Country Bicycle Rout Readied for '76 Tourists," *Christian Science Monitor*, September 3, 1974, 1.
165. "History on the Rails," *Time*, November 25, 1974, 12.
166. Hollie I. West, "A Bicentennial Exhibit for Overseas," *Washington Post*, November 26, 1974, B3.

167. West, "Bicentennial Exhibit."
168. Stephanie Slahor, "Try Colonial Living in Your Home," *Christian Science Monitor*, December 3, 1974, 20.
169. "The Power of the People," *Christian Science Monitor*, December 5, 1974, 18.
170. "Power of the People."
171. Stephen Webbe, "Avoiding a Bicentennial Traffic Jam of Millions," *Christian Science Monitor*, December 16, 1974, 4.
172. Webbe, "Avoiding a Bicentennial Traffic Jam."
173. "Ford to Name Bicentennial Agency Aide," *Washington Post*, October 3, 1974, A35.
174. James T. Wooten, "A British Born Woman Is Appointed to No. 2 in Bicentennial Agency," *New York Times*, October 3, 1974, 18.
175. Frederick M. Winship, "Bicentennial Stirs Grass Roots," *Atlanta Constitution*, November 17, 1974, 10C.
176. Winship, "Bicentennial Stirs Grass Roots."
177. Winship, "Bicentennial Stirs Grass Roots."
178. Winship, "Bicentennial Stirs Grass Roots."
179. Winship, "Bicentennial Stirs Grass Roots."
180. Winship, "Bicentennial Stirs Grass Roots."
181. Winship, "Bicentennial Stirs Grass Roots."
182. Don McLeod, "Bicentennial Heads Seek Additional Funds," *Austin American-Statesman*, December 13, 1974, A46.
183. McLeod, "Bicentennial Heads Seek Additional Funds."
184. Margot Hornblower, "Ford Talks About Train for Freedom," *Washington Post*, December 20, 1974, C1.
185. Hornblower, "Ford Talks About Train."

Chapter 3

186. Margot Hornblower, "Bicentennial Fever Spreads Across U.S," *Washington Post*, February 16, 1975, 1.
187. Margot Hornblower, "Minorities to Meet on U.S. Fete," *Washington Post*, January 20, 1975, C1.
188. Gloria C. Oden, "It's About Time," *Essence*, January 1975, 8.
189. Delores C. Leffall, "The Bicentennial and the Afro-American: A Selected Bibliography," *Negro History Bulletin*, February/March 1975, 358–61.
190. William L. Patterson, "The Bicentennial of a Racist State," *Louisville Defender*, March 6, 1975, B9.
191. "Gregory Turns Sights from War to U.S. Rehabilitation," *Jet*, May 22, 1975, 64.

192. "Bicentennial Show to Depict Black Americans," *Atlanta Daily World*, March 23, 1975, 6.
193. "Map Black Role in Bicentennial Fete," *Chicago Defender*, April 1, 1975, 21.
194. "Bicentennial Exhibit Takes to U.S. Rails," *Atlanta Daily World*, April 4, 1975, 1.
195. Darcelle Kanoyton, "There's Something for All in Upcoming Bicentennial," *Michigan Chronicle*, May 10, 1975, C1.
196. James P. Murray, "The Bicentennial Dilemma for Blacks Is…," *New York Amsterdam News*, June 4, 1975, B10.
197. "Don't Forget the Blacks Bicentennial Boards Told," *Jet*, June 19, 1975, 6.
198. Elizabeth Hood, "Blacks and the Bicentennial," *Michigan Chronicle*, June 21, 1975, 11.
199. "Brainstorming the Bicentennial," *History News*, January 1975, 4.
200. Hornblower, "Bicentennial Fever Spreads."
201. Marilyn Hoffman, "Bicentennial May Boost Antiques…," *Christian Science Monitor*, January 21, 1975, 11.
202. Margaret Daly, "Can You Make Money with Your Crafts?," *Better Homes and Gardens*, January 1975, 24.
203. Margot Hornblower, "Parade, Exhibits Inaugurate Bicentennial Conference," *Washington Post*, February 25, 1975, C1.
204. Clayton Jones, "Do-It-Yourself Bicentennial Plans," *Christian Science Monitor*, March 5, 1975, 1.
205. Jones, "Do-It-Yourself Bicentennial Plans."
206. Jones, "Do-It-Yourself Bicentennial Plans."
207. Jones, "Do-It-Yourself Bicentennial Plans."
208. "NAACP Joins on Bicentennial," *Los Angeles Sentinel*, March 6, 1975, A2.
209. William H. Stringer, "Americans' Reasons to Celebrate," *Christian Science Monitor*, March 7, 1975, 7.
210. William H. Stringer, "After 200 Years—What Is America?," *Christian Science Monitor*, April 4, 1975, 28.
211. Phyllis Hanes, "Elegant Period Food," *Christian Science Monitor*, April 17, 1975, 19.
212. Philip Shabecoff, "Ford, on Bicentennial Trip, Bids U.S. Heed Old Values," *New York Times*, April 19, 1975, 1.
213. "The U.S. Begins Its Birthday Bash," *Time*, April 21, 1975.
214. Alexandra Johnson, "Biographies Bloom Under Bicentennial Sun," *Christian Science Monitor*, April 23, 1975, 26.
215. Janet Domowitz, "Authors Harken to Rumbles of 1776," *Christian Science Monitor*, May 28, 1975, 30.
216. "Bicentennial Programming: Plans, Crafts, Authors," *Library Journal* (June 1975): 1181–182.
217. Daniel J. Boorstin, "America: Our Byproduct Nation," *Time*, June 23, 1975.

218. "Untitled," *Time*, June 23, 1975.
219. Leavitt F. Morris, "Mickey, Goofy, Donald Romp-Bicentennial Style," *Christian Science Monitor*, July 8, 1975, 21.
220. Morris, "Mickey, Goofy, Donald Romp."
221. "Pocketful of History," *Time*, July 14, 1975.
222. "Postal Service Announces Bicentennial Stamp Issue," *Christian Science Monitor*, September 16, 1975, 30.
223. Charles E. Price, "Bicentennial Celebration for Us, Too," *Atlanta Daily World*, July 10, 1975, 4.
224. Richard L. Strout, "Slavery and the Founding Fathers," *Christian Science Monitor*, July 11, 1975, 32.
225. "Ebony Planning Bicentennial Issue," *Chicago Defender*, August 2, 1975, 7.
226. Arthur Zebbs, "Bicentennial: So What?," *Cleveland Call and Post*, August 16, 1975, 28.
227. "Blacks Speak Out on Bicentennial Celebration," *Pittsburgh Courier*, July 19, 1975, 4.
228. "Bicentennial Backs Women, Minorities," *New York Times*, July 20, 1975, 38.
229. "Name Committee of Minorities to Advise in Bicentennial," *Chicago Defender*, August 11, 1975, 7.
230. "Ethnic Groups Urged to Plan Activities for Bicentennial," *Chicago Defender*, August 18, 1975, 5.
231. "Bicentennial Lectures Planned," *American Israelite*, August 28, 1975, 14.
232. James A. Cobb, "Blacks Bicentennial," *Michigan Chronicle*, September 27, 1975, 9.
233. Mary Lynn, "Bicentennial Exhibition Features Black History," *Cleveland Call and Post*, October 11, 1975, 11B.
234. "Harlem Inst. Presents Bicentennial Fashions by Black Designers," *Philadelphia Tribune*, October 18, 1975, 9.
235. "Festivals," *Seventeen*, July 1975, 46.
236. "Public Radio Network Creates Program for Bicentennial Interest," *History News* (July 1975): 159–60.
237. Arthur Unger, "A Look Ahead at NBC's Bicentennial Specials," *Christian Science Monitor*, July 24, 1975, 29.
238. George Moneyhun, "U.S. Uniformmakers Never Had It So Good," *Christian Science Monitor*, July 28, 1978, 1.
239. Cecelia K. Toth, "The Official Bicentennial Quilt," *Good Housekeeping*, July 1975, 84.
240. Byron Rosen, "NFL Enters Bicentennial Act with Shoulder Emblem, Essay," *Washington Post*, August 5, 1975, D3.
241. Constance Holden, "The Bicentennial: Science Loses Out," *Science*, August 8, 1975, 438.

242. Bruno Bitker, "A Way to Celebrate the Bicentennial," *American Bar Association Journal* 61, no. 8 (August 1975): 941–44.
243. Bernard Hunt, "Foreigners Cashing in on '76," *Washington Post*, August 13, 1975, A10.
244. Hunt, "Foreigners Cashing in on '76."
245. Lucia Mouat, "Bicentennial Sales Galloping," *Christian Science Monitor*, September 5, 1975, 2.
246. "Bucks from the Bicentennial," *Time*, September 29, 1975.
247. Mouat, "Bicentennial Sales Galloping."
248. Millicent Taylor, "Bicentennial Adds Color to Bulb Selections for '76," *Christian Science Monitor*, September 5, 1975, 25.
249. Marilyn Hoffman, "American Folk Art Boosted by Bicentennial," *Christian Science Monitor*, October 14, 1975, 37.
250. "Tourists and the Bicentennial," *Los Angeles Sentinel*, September 11, 1975, 18.
251. Margot Hornblower, "27 Million D.C. Tourists Forecast for Bicentennial," *Washington Post*, December 5, 1975, B1.
252. Barbara Fertig, "We, the People. At the National Museum of History and Technology, Through the Bicentennial Years," *Roundtable Reports*, October 1975.
253. Clayton Jones, "Time Bombs for the Tricentennial," *Christian Science Monitor*, November 5, 1975, 2.
254. "BiCentennial Con Game," *Louisville Defender*, November 13, 1975, B7.
255. "Heritage Thanksgiving," *Better Homes and Gardens*, November 1975, 114.
256. James A. Beard, "Tribute-to-America Thanksgiving," *Woman's Day*, November 1975, 65.
257. "Spirits of '76," *Ladies' Home Journal*, December 1975, 84–85, 94.
258. Bess Myerson, "Call to Action: The National Women's Agenda," *Redbook*, November 1975, 71.
259. Margot Hornblower, "Slogan Contest Gets Big Results," *Washington Post*, December 16, 1975, B5.
260. Hornblower, "Slogan Contest Gets Big Results."
261. "'The Great American History Test,'" *Chicago Defender*, December 8, 1975, 21.
262. Aretha Watkins, "Cass Senior State Winner in Bicentennial Contest," *Michigan Chronicle*, December 20, 1975, 1.
263. Bernice Shelton, "What Is to Become of the Bicentennial?," *Baltimore Afro-American*, October 18, 1975, 12.
264. "Bicentennial Program to Mark Contribution Sites Set," *New Pittsburgh Courier*, October 25, 1975, 2.
265. "Bicen Projects Listed," *Baltimore Afro-American*, December 20, 1975, 5.

266. Nadine Brown, "Blacks Role in City History Urged During Bicentennial," *Michigan Chronicle*, October 25, 1975, A1.
267. Marie Teasley, "Contributions to the Bicentennial," *Michigan Chronicle*, November 15, 1975, 7C.
268. "Widow of Dr. W.E.B. DuBois Cites Stake in Bicentennial," *Chicago Defender*, November 10, 1975, 4.
269. Prentis Rogers, "Freedom Struggle Called Real Story of Bicentennial," *Atlanta Daily World*, November 16, 1975, 1.
270. "Jordan Notes Inequality as Bicentennial Nears," *Chicago Defender*, December 4, 1975, 2.
271. Father Lawrence E. Lucas, "More on Blacks and the Bicentennial," *New York Amsterdam News*, December 20, 1975, A7.
272. Benjamin E. Mays, "Our Bicentennial," *Chicago Defender*, December 27, 1975, 4.

Chapter 4

273. Margot Hornblower, "National Chain of Hands Suggested for Bicentennial," *Washington Post*, January 14, 1976, A4.
274. Hornblower, "National Chain of Hands Suggested."
275. Hornblower, "National Chain of Hands Suggested."
276. Peter C. Stuart, "Bloated U.S. Government: Target for 1976 'Revolt,'" *Christian Science Monitor*, January 5, 1976, 5.
277. Roderick Nordell, "Voices of America: Coast to Coast to Find the Spirit of 1976," *Christian Science Monitor*, January 5, 1976, 14.
278. "It's Official—1976 Is Our Bicentennial," *UPI*, January 8, 1976.
279. "Random Notes," *Rolling Stone*, January 15, 1976, 21.
280. "'Sesame Street' Has Bicentennial Fun," *Chicago Defender*, January 15, 1976, 25.
281. "Four Faith Groups Plan TV Programs," *Norfolk Journal and Guide*, January 17, 1976, 13; "Religious Groups to Air Bicentennial TV Specials," *Jet*, January 22, 1976, 14.
282. "Horse Favored in Bicentennial Vote," *Norfolk New Journal and Guide*, January 24, 1976, 8.
283. Will Lissner, "Save the U.S. Bicentennial," *American Journal of Economics and Sociology* 35, no. 4 (October 1976): 48.
284. Clayton Jones, "Star-Spangled Knickknacks Threaten Bicentennial," *Christian Science Monitor*, February 3, 1976, 1.
285. Margot Hornblower, "Bicentennial Ripoff," *Washington Post*, February 8, 1976, 3.
286. Jones, "Star-Spangled Knickknacks."
287. Jones, "Star-Spangled Knickknacks."

288. "Schools Begin Bicentennial Observance," *Hartford Courant*, February 6, 1976, 20.
289. Lin Hilburn, "Bicentennial and the Real Spirit of America," *Los Angeles Sentinel*, January 8, 1976, A7.
290. Vashti McKenzie, "Blacks and the Televised Bicentennial Celebrations," *Baltimore Afro-American*, January 24, 1976, 11.
291. Joseph Carpenter, "The Bicentennial and the Black Revolution: Is It a Myth or a Reality?," *Negro History Bulletin*, January 1976, 496.
292. Elmer Eugene Wells, "What Can Blacks Celebrate During Bicentennial Year?," *Negro History Bulletin*, January 1976, 501.
293. "1976 Black History Week Expanded to Month-Long Bicentennial Celebration," *Jet*, February 5, 1976, 25.
294. "Smithsonian Tours Take Bicentennial Over Nation," *New Pittsburgh Courier*, February 14, 1976, 40.
295. Associated Press, "Students Explore Teepee Life," *Christian Science Monitor*, February 23, 1976, 20.
296. "Bicentennial Rally Set by Ku Klux Klan," *Atlanta Daily World*, March 4, 1976, 7.
297. "Bicentennial Projects Awarded Grants," *Washington Post*, March 25, 1976, D.C.6.
298. Doris Eby and Nancy Byal, "America: The Melting Pot of Good Cooking," *Better and Gardens*, March 1976, 84.
299. "Bicentennial Tribute to Black Americans Set," *Atlanta Daily Word*, April 13, 1976, 2.
300. Margot Hornblower, "Home-Grown Celebrations and…," *Washington Post*, February 8, 1976, 109.
301. Stewart Dill McBride, "Boston Mulls Tourist Spirit of '76," *Christian Science Monitor*, February 9, 1976, B13.
302. Jack Miner, "Sailing Out of History—A Bicentennial Armada," *Christian Science Monitor*, February 24, 1976, 12.
303. Diana Loercher, "Bicentennial Bounty at N.Y.'s Met," *Christian Science Monitor*, February 26, 1976, 27.
304. "Philadelphia: The Bicentennial City," *American Bar Association Journal* 62, no. 2 (February 1976): 201.
305. Peter C. Stuart, "Washington Dresses Up for Bicentennial Invasion," *Christian Science Monitor*, April 5, 1976, 1.
306. "200-Years of Celebration in Boston and Washington," *Redbook*, March 1976, R-3.
307. "Armed Forces Bicentennial Caravan Here," *Norfolk New Journal and Guide*, April 10, 1976, 11.
308. "A Happy 200th Birthday, Uncle Sam," *Time*, April 12, 1976.
309. Clayton Jones, "July 4 Fireworks: How Safe Rockets' Red Glare?," *Christian Science Monitor*, April 15, 1976, 3.

310. Jack Eisen, "July 4 Extravaganza Set," *Washington Post*, April 15, 1976, A1.
311. Sally Quinn, "John Warner: Rally Round the Flag," *Washington Post*, April 16, 1976, B1.
312. "Hookers to Converge on Washington, D.C.," *Jet*, May 20, 1976.
313. James M. Banner, "Why the Bicentennial?," *Washington Post*, April 18, 1976, B1.
314. Banner, "Why the Bicentennial."
315. "Hilton to Initiate Daily Bicentennial Flag Salute," *Atlanta Daily World*, May 2, 1976, 10.
316. Paul Hodge, "'Bikecentennial' Will Begin Along 4,250-Mile Route," *Washington Post*, May 10, 1976, B1.
317. Lucia Mouat, "Americans to Hit the Road for Bicentennial Vacations," *Christian Science Monitor*, May 11, 1976, 1.
318. Leavitt F. Morris, "Mystic Seaport Visitors Will Think This Is 1876," *Christian Science Monitor*, May 11, 1976, 25.
319. Samuel A. Tower, "Stamps," *New York Times*, May 23, 1976, X42.
320. F.R. Bruns, "United States Postal Service Issues," *Washington Post*, June 20, 1976, H7.
321. Diane Perkins, "Bicentennial Lures Visitors to U.S.," *Christian Science Monitor*, June 28, 1976, 2.
322. Jack Miner, "Operation Sail—Where to See the Tall Ships," *Christian Science Monitor*, June 28, 1976, 14.
323. Felix Gilbert, "Bicentennial Reflections," *Foreign Affairs*, July 1976, 635–44.
324. "The Birthday Spirit," *Time*, July 5, 1976, 50.
325. David E. Anderson, "Pope's Bicentennial Message Praises American Catholics," *UPI*, June 26, 1976, 21.
326. Gerald R. Ford, "A Special Message from President Gerald R. Ford," *Saturday Evening Post*, July/August 1976, 132.
327. "The Big 200th Bash," *Time*, July 5, 1976, 8.
328. "Big 200th Bash."
329. "Big 200th Bash."
330. "Big 200th Bash."
331. "Hooray for that Old RWB," *Time*, July 5, 1976, 66.
332. Stewart Dill McBride and Celia Herron, "The Parade of Weekend Activities," *Christian Science Monitor*, June 29, 1976, 12.
333. McBride and Herron, "Parade of Weekend Activities."
334. "The Birthday Spirit," *Time*, July 5, 1976, 50.
335. Eileen Miller, "Bicentennial Bonsai," *Science and Children*, October 1976, 27.
336. "The Iron Within," *Time*, July 12, 1976, 8.
337. John Beaufort, "Bicentennial Playback," *Christian Science Monitor*, July 15, 1976, 27.

338. Hugh Sydney, "A Feeling of People Together," *Time*, July 19, 1976, 27.
339. Vernon E. Jordan, "To Be Equal: A Better Way to Observe the Bicentennial," *Baltimore Afro-American*, July 31, 1976, 4.
340. Alvin Kogut, "Reflections on the Bicentennial," *Social Work*, July 1976, 263.
341. Linn Washington, "Bicentennial Celebration Falls Short of Millions—Money and People," *Philadelphia Tribune*, December 25, 1976, 20.
342. Washington, "Bicentennial Celebration Falls Short."
343. Mike Causey, "Bicentennial Unit Writes Swan Song," *Washington Post*, June 21, 1976, C2.
344. Sandra G. Boodman, "Souvenir Strategy: Bidding Bye-Bye to the Buy-Centennial," *Washington Post*, August 1, 1976, 121.
345. Howard Coffin, "Vermonters Disappointed: Where Are All the Tourists?," *Christian Science Monitor*, August 5, 1976, 10.
346. Bernice Shelton, "Bicentennial Traffic Continuous in Philly," *Baltimore Afro-American*, August 7, 1976, 12.
347. "$2 Bills Becoming a Bicentennial Bust: FRB," *Jet*, September 16, 1976, 46.
348. U.S. Bureau of Education, *Report of the Commissioner of Education for 1875* (U.S. Government Printing Office, 1876), xii.
349. John Berry, "Bye-Bye Bicentennial," *Library Journal*, November 1976, 2207.
350. Georgia E. Ireland, "Blacks and the Bicentennial in New England," *New York Amsterdam News*, June 26, 1976, A9A.
351. "Thanksgiving in Plymouth Puts Spotlight on Early Black Colonial Settlement," *Jet*, December 2, 1976, 53.
352. "Parting Ways Cemetery," See Plymouth Massachusetts, https://seeplymouth.com/listing/parting-ways-cemetery/.
353. Karl F. Heiffer, "Black Cemetery on Long Island Becomes Focus of Bicentennial," *New York Amsterdam News*, June 26, 1976, D7A.
354. "Party's Ending for Bicentennial," *Atlanta Constitution*, December 19, 1976, 15C.
355. "Party's Ending for Bicentennial."
356. "Party's Ending for Bicentennial."
357. Susan Page, "'The Bicentennial Is Over, You Know,'" *Newsday*, December 26, 1976, 6.
358. Page, "'Bicentennial Is Over.'"
359. Page, "'Bicentennial Is Over.'"
360. "At the Bicentennial: 'Moral Realism' Is the Mood of the Country," *The Hastings Center Report*, December 1976, 2.
361. Page, "'Bicentennial Is Over.'"
362. Page, "'Bicentennial Is Over.'"

363. "That Bicentennial Year," *Christian Science Monitor*, December 28, 1976, 20.
364. "That Bicentennial Year."

Epilogue

365. "President Ford Narrates Bicentennial Minute," *Chicago Defender*, January 1, 1977, 1, 8.
366. Lance Carden, "Tide of Bicentennial Visitors Left Some Sites a Mite Dry," *Christian Science Monitor*, January 6, 1977, 5.
367. "Notes and Comments," *The New Yorker*, January 3, 1977, 18.
368. "How We Proudly Hailed a Most Glorious 4th," *Life*, January 17, 1977.
369. "Urban League Cites a Bicentennial 'Bust,'" *Chicago Defender*, March 16, 1977, 24.
370. John W. Warner, "The Rediscovery of America," *Saturday Evening Post*, April 1977, 12, 80.
371. Warner, "Rediscovery of America."
372. Warner, "Rediscovery of America."
373. "Bicentennial Panel Closing Its Doors," *Los Angeles Times*, June 26, 1977, A12.
374. Andrew Glass, "Festival for 200th Anniversary of Constitutional Convention, May 23, 1987," Politico, May 23, 2013, https://www.politico.com/story/2013/05/festival-for-200th-anniversary-of-constitutional-convention-may-23-1987-091771.
375. "America's 250th Birthday Party Starts Early in Philly. Here's What to Expect Over Next 2 Years," NBC Philadelphia, https://www.nbcphiladelphia.com/news/local/america-250th-anniversary-philadelphia/3863989/.

Selected Bibliography

Bailey, Beth and David Farber, eds. *America in the Seventies.* University Press of Kansas, 2004.

Beard, Charles. *An Economic Interpretation of the Constitution.* Macmillan, 1913.

Bodnar, John. *Remaking America: Public Memory, Commemoration, and Patriotism in the Twentieth Century.* Princeton University Press, 1991.

Gilberti, Bruno. *Designing the Centennial: A History of the 1876 International Exhibition in Philadelphia.* University Press of Kentucky, 2021.

Gordon, Tammy S. *The Spirit of 1976: Commerce, Community, and the Politics of Commemoration.* University of Massachusetts Press, 2013.

Gross, Linda P., and Theresa R. Snyder. *Philadelphia's 1876 Centennial Exhibition.* Arcadia Publishing, 2005.

Hartje, Robert J. *Bicentennial USA: Pathways to Celebration.* American Association for State and Local History, 1973.

Myrdal, Gunnar. *An American Dilemma: The Negro Problem and Modern Democracy*. Harper & Brothers, 1944.

Rockefeller, John D., III *The Second American Revolution: Some Personal Observations*. HarperCollins, 1973.

Rymsza-Pawlowska, M.J. *History Comes Alive: Public History and Popular Culture in the 1970s*. University of North Carolina Press, 2017.

Samuel, Lawrence R. *The End of the Innocence: The 1964-1965 New York World's Fair*. Syracuse University Press, 2007.

———. *Pledging Allegiance: American Identity and the Bond Drive of World War II*. Smithsonian Institution Press, 1997.

U.S. Bureau of Education. *Report of the Commissioner of Education for 1875*. U.S. Government Printing Office, 1876.

Image Credits

3 Photographer: Bernard Gotfryd. Courtesy of the Library of Congress. https://www.loc.gov/item/2020736372/.

23 LEFT: Courtesy of the Gerald R. Ford Presidential Library & Museum. Accession Number: 1983.24.

23 RIGHT: Courtesy of the Gerald R. Ford Presidential Library & Museum. Accession Number: 1981.43.

30 Caldwell, Jacquie Ursula, Artist, and Sponsor/Advertiser Wages For Housework,1976. Courtesy of the Library of Congress. https://www.loc.gov/item/2016648549/.

46 National Archives. Local Identifier: 64-NA-5082.

47 National Archives Identifier: 35810744. Local Identifier: 64-NA-5667.

62 Courtesy of the Library of Congress. https://www.loc.gov/item/2024630366/.

65 Photographer: Warren K. Leffler. Courtesy of the Library of Congress. https://www.loc.gov/item/2024630439/.

73 Museums found creative ways to connect their respective collections to the Bicentennial. Courtesy of the Library of Congress. https://www.loc.gov/item/2014649585/.

75 Courtesy of the Library of Congress. https://www.loc.gov/item/2024630164/.

86 Courtesy of the Library of Congress. https://www.loc.gov/item/2024630165/.

87 Photographer: Marion S. Trikosko. Courtesy of the Library of Congress. https://www.loc.gov/item/2024630174/.

92 Courtesy of the Library of Congress. https://www.loc.gov/item/2024630163/.
93 Photographer: Warren K. Leffler. Courtesy of the Library of Congress. https://www.loc.gov/item/2024630172/.
102 Courtesy of the Library of Congress. https://www.loc.gov/item/2015649606/.
104 Robinson, Beverly J. Courtesy of the Library of Congress. https://www.loc.gov/item/awhbib000050/.
105 NAID: 30805973 Local ID: GRF-WHPO-B2233-14A National Archives Catalog.
112 TOP: Smithsonian Institution Archives. Accession Number: 94-123, National Museum of American History. Division of Political History, Exhibition Records.
112 BOTTOM: Photographer: Marion S. Trikosko. Courtesy of the Library of Congress. https://www.loc.gov/item/2024630305/.
118 Artist: Maret Maiste. Courtesy of the Library of Congress. https://www.loc.gov/item/2016649204/.
135 National Archives Identifier: 35810684. Local Identifier: 64-NA-5623.
137 TOP: Courtesy of the Gerald R. Ford Presidential Library & Museum. Accession Number: 1990.147.
137 BOTTOM LEFT: Courtesy of the Gerald R. Ford Presidential Library & Museum. Accession Number: 1988.916.2.
137 BOTTOM RIGHT: Courtesy of the Gerald R. Ford Presidential Library & Museum. Accession Number: 1988.1173.
138 TOP: Courtesy of the Gerald R. Ford Presidential Library & Museum. Accession Number: 1989.432.1.
138 BOTTOM: Courtesy of the Gerald R. Ford Presidential Library & Museum. Accession Number: 1989.636.1.
139 TOP: Courtesy of the Gerald R. Ford Presidential Library & Museum. Accession Number: 1982.88.
139 BOTTOM LEFT: Courtesy of the Gerald R. Ford Presidential Library & Museum. Accession Number: 2004.563.1 a-b.
139 BOTTOM RIGHT: Courtesy of the Gerald R. Ford Presidential Library & Museum. Accession Number: 2007.179.3.
140 TOP LEFT: Courtesy of the Gerald R. Ford Presidential Library & Museum. No accession number.
140 TOP RIGHT: Courtesy of the Gerald R. Ford Presidential Library & Museum. Accession Number: 1988.16.2.
140 BOTTOM: Courtesy of the Gerald R. Ford Presidential Library & Museum. Accession Number: 1988.59.
141 TOP: Courtesy of the Gerald R. Ford Presidential Library & Museum. Accession Number: 2006.41.

141 BOTTOM: Courtesy of the Gerald R. Ford Presidential Library & Museum. Accession Number: 1983.96.
142 TOP: Courtesy of the Gerald R. Ford Presidential Library & Museum. Accession Number: 1988.208.
142 BOTTOM: Courtesy of the Gerald R. Ford Presidential Library & Museum. Accession Number: 2004.570.
143 TOP LEFT: Courtesy of the Gerald R. Ford Presidential Library & Museum. Accession Number: 1987.752.
143 BOTTOM LEFT: Courtesy of the Gerald R. Ford Presidential Library & Museum. Accession Number: 1988.920.2.
143 RIGHT: Courtesy of the Gerald R. Ford Presidential Library & Museum. Accession Number: 1988.63.
149 Courtesy of the Gerald R. Ford Presidential Library & Museum. Photographer: William Fitz-Patrick. July 7, 1976. Image: B0549-30.
150 Photographer: Thomas J. O'Halloran. Courtesy of the Library of Congress. https://www.loc.gov/item/2024630146/.
152 Courtesy of the Gerald R. Ford Presidential Library & Museum. Photographer: David Hume Kennerly. July 4, 1976. Image: B0510-35.
153 Courtesy of the Gerald R. Ford Presidential Library & Museum. Photographer: David Hume Kennerly. July 4th, 1976. Image: B0513-07A.
154 Courtesy of the Gerald R. Ford Presidential Library & Museum. Photographer: Karl Schumacher. July 4, 1976. Image: B0493-15.
157 Courtesy of the Library of Congress. https://www.loc.gov/item/2020734366/.
158 Photographer: Bernard Gotfryd. Courtesy of the Library of Congress. https://www.loc.gov/item/2020734387/.
160 Courtesy of the Library of Congress. https://www.loc.gov/item/2019630947/.
162 Courtesy of the Gerald R. Ford Presidential Library & Museum. Photographer: William Fitz-Patrick. July 5, 1976. Image: B0522-07.
172 Photographer: Marion S. Trikosko. Courtesy of the Library of Congress. https://www.loc.gov/item/2024630169/.
176 Photographer: Bernard Gotfryd. Courtesy of the Library of Congress. https://www.loc.gov/item/2020736371/.

About the Author

LAWRENCE R. SAMUEL is a Miami – and New York City – based cultural historian. He holds a PhD in American studies and an MA in English from the University of Minnesota and an MBA in marketing from the University of Georgia and was a Smithsonian Institution Fellow. His previous books include *Tudor City: Manhattan's Historic Residential Enclave* (2019); *Dead on Arrival in Manhattan: Stories of Unnatural Demise from the Past Century* (2021); and *Making Long Island: A History of Growth and the American Dream* (2023).